Praise

Entrepreneurship provides an exciting new career for millions of older Americans—one they would never have anticipated growing up in a world that presumed people's work life would end at 65. Rick Terrien has provided a fabulous roadmap on how to approach this new chapter in life. His brilliant *Ageless Startup* is a handbook for how to shape your future so your most rewarding work lies ahead—work that benefits you and makes a difference in the lives of countless others. A must for career planning for anyone over forty!

—CARL SCHRAMM, FORMER PRESIDENT OF THE KAUFFMAN FOUNDATION, AUTHOR OF *BURN THE BUSINESS PLAN*, SERIAL ENTREPRENEUR, ACTIVE VENTURE INVESTOR, AND PROFESSOR AT SYRACUSE UNIVERSITY

Ageless Startup focuses on a critically important but often ignored topic, which is the emerging "next career" for a growing segment of our population—the 40 to 65 age cohort. Rick Terrien shines a spotlight on this growing segment with timeless advice as an experienced entrepreneur. There is much for us to learn about the ongoing journey of entrepreneurship that knows no boundaries, no age limit, or no career/life stage barrier. I applaud Rick for this important and necessary read.

—AUDREY J. MURRELL, PH.D., PROFESSOR AND DEAN OF UNIVERSITY OF PITTSBURGH, HONORS COLLEGE

I love, love, love Rick Terrien's myth-busting book *Ageless Startup* where research shows that it's the 50-year-old—not the 20-year-old—who is more likely to start a successful business. *Ageless Startup* puts entrepreneurship back on the table as a potential income opportunity for older adults. It is a must-read, offering step-by-step guidance on how to start and grow your own business.

—ELIZABETH WHITE, AUTHOR OF *55, UNDEREMPLOYED, AND FAKING NORMAL*

With *Ageless Startup*, Rick Terrien has managed to make the book a fun read while providing practical, useful advice in a voice that is clear and supportive.

—Karen Fulbright-Anderson, Ph.D., CEO of
Fulbright-Anderson and Associates

Ageless Startup takes Rick Terrien's decades of entrepreneurial know-how and channels it into a guide to help other "ageless innovators" on their journey. Along the way, he shares tips from dozens of inspiring social entrepreneurs making their biggest impact in the second half of life as they work to create a better future for all. If you're committed to pursuing later-life creativity and innovation, you'll find a kindred spirit in Rick!

—Eunice Lin Nichols, vice president and Gen2Gen co-chair, encore.org

You have wisdom and maturity and, now with this book, you have the inside tactics you need to succeed at any age. Highly recommended, especially if you're over 50.

— Dr. Joe Vitale, author of *Zero Limits* and *The Miracle*

This book shares valuable how-to tips to start small, smart, and slow. If you see yourself embracing the exciting journey of entrepreneurship in the second half of life, delay no further and take the first step by reading this life-changing book.

—Sharon Gregory, entrepreneur, Six Sigma Master Black Belt, founder and president of Hexagon Solutions and Beyond

If you have experienced a loss of purpose, interest, or direction during middle-age or senior years, this book is a must read. Rick Terrien demonstrates the value in starting again and writing your own new chapter. He not only reveals the secret to discovering and igniting a new passion, but also how to ensure your renewed purpose uplifts others and changes communities.

—Gregg Kander, Esq., 2019 Purpose Prize Fellow and general counsel for Sweet'N Low/Sugar in the Raw

The business world would be a much more efficient, compassionate, and regenerative space if we conducted ourselves as Rick does. *Ageless Startup* represents the best of Rick's entrepreneurial guidance.

—MATT D'AMOUR, ENTREPRENEUR AND HOLISTIC LIFESTYLE COACH

After picking up a copy of *Ageless Startup*, I realized this was a game changer! You're never too old to find new ways to leave your mark on the world, and I would highly recommend *Ageless Startup* as the perfect roadmap to turning your dreams into reality at any age!

—RUSS ROBERTS, EXECUTIVE DIRECTOR OF WAUKESHA COUNTY TECHNICAL COLLEGE SMALL BUSINESS CENTER

Ageless Startup has been a vital guidebook as I transition from paid employment into entrepreneurship. Rick Terrien's book is a roadmap for giving yourself permission to explore entrepreneurship in the second half of life.

—JOY GIESEKE, ENTREPRENEUR AND YARN ENTHUSIAST

Ageless Startup brings attention and merit to a critical topic—capitalizing on your entrepreneurial spirit after the age of 45. Rick does a tremendous job of helping the reader understand why the entrepreneurial spirit is time-proof.

—WAYNE JONES, ED.D., CEO OF PENN HILLS CHARTER SCHOOL OF ENTREPRENEURSHIP

Amidst the incessant din comes a wise book that speaks directly to those with a lifetime of knowledge, skills, networks, and a little available money. *Ageless Startup* helps us reflect on how we can leverage that into something that can produce a source of income and make the world a better place.

—GREGG R. BAKER, TENURED AND COMMISSIONED U.S. FOREIGN SERVICE OFFICER WITH USAID AND CHIEF ECONOMIST FOR USAID PROGRAMS

Rick's book is right on time for entrepreneurs.

—BILL HARRISON, CO-OWNER, BRADLEY COMMUNICATIONS CORP.

This book strikes me as absolutely the right message at the right time.
Rick's real-world experience and knowledge come through, and as I
learned fighting cancer almost 20 years ago, knowledge kills fear.

—MICHAEL HOADLEY, CCIM, PMP, AND DIRECTOR OF REAL ESTATE AT
GLIDEPATH POWER SOLUTIONS

Rick's real-world wisdom and guidance show how to galvanize your
life experience and finally break the wheel of discontentment.
The result: unlocking the success behind what you want to do,
not what you "should."

—DAVE KWASNICK, CLIO ONE SHOW AND AMERICAN ADVERTISING
FEDERATION NATIONAL AWARD WINNER

Start
a Business at
Any Age

AGELESS
STARTUP

Rick Terrien

Entrepreneur Press®

Entrepreneur Press, Publisher
Cover Design: Andrew Welyczko
Production and Composition: Eliot House Productions

This publication is designed to provide accurate and authoritative information in regard to the subject matter covered. It is sold with the understanding that the publisher is not engaged in rendering legal, accounting, or other professional services. If legal advice or other expert assistance is required, the services of a competent professional person should be sought.

Entrepreneur Press® is a registered trademark of Entrepreneur Media, Inc.

Library of Congress Cataloging-in-Publication Data
Names: Terrien, Rick, author.
Title: Ageless startup : start a business at any age / Rick Terrien.
Description: Irvine, CA : Entrepreneur Press, [2020] | Includes index. | Summary: "Ageless Startup guides retirees through the world of entrepreneurship. The book discusses what it takes to start a business at an advanced age, how seniors set themselves apart from their younger competitors, and provides general business startup guidance"-- Provided by publisher.
Identifiers: LCCN 2020000616 (print) | LCCN 2020000617 (ebook) | ISBN 978-1-59918-663-4 (paperback) | ISBN 978-1-61308-420-5 (ebook)
Subjects: LCSH: New business enterprises. | Retirees--Employment. | Older people--Employment. | Entrepreneurship.
Classification: LCC HD62.5 .T474 2020 (print) | LCC HD62.5 (ebook) | DDC 658.1/1--dc23
LC record available at https://lccn.loc.gov/2020000616
LC ebook record available at https://lccn.loc.gov/2020000617

Printed in the United States of America

24 23 22 21 20   10 9 8 7 6 5 4 3 2 1

CONTENTS

FOREWORD

By John Golden

Assistant professor, entrepreneur-in-residence, and managing director of the Sustainable Enterprise Accelerator at Slippery Rock University

I t's been almost thirty years since I took my son and daughter, then ages six and four, ice skating for the very first time. We travelled to a local ice arena, and I rented small-sized skates, which I fastened snugly on their feet. I remember giving them some small words of caution. Before I could tie on my own skates, my kids jumped from the bleachers onto the ice and began skating at full speed. I watched with fright and amazement, wondering how they would stop safely. But stop they did. They hit the wall at the corner of the ice arena, fell to the ice laughing, got up, and began skating off in another direction. Didn't they understand that it was necessary to learn the established techniques by taking small steps onto the ice? Why didn't they wait for my experienced instruction? How did they think they were going to stop? Weren't they afraid of getting hurt?

Remember when you were a kid? Remember when you would take chances without fully understanding all of the possible outcomes? Remember feeling like you could do anything you wanted and weren't afraid to try? In *Ageless Startup*, Rick Terrien, a lifelong entrepreneur, helps us reconnect to the kid that still lives in each of us. He reminds us that the penchant for risk-taking never really disappears, but becomes buried underneath a pile of jobs, raising children, paying mortgages, and planning for retirement. Rick understands that for many of us, "today" soon becomes "maybe someday." And he also understands our fears that the "someday" may never come. But Rick says, "Don't wait. Your new enterprise is out there to start and grow. What's in it for you? Maybe nothing. Maybe something. Maybe the stars."

Ageless Startup takes us back, lifts us up over our fears, and then moves us forward. It teaches us that we need not conform to the demographic expectations of our physical age. It reminds us, however, that this time around we are more thoughtful, more authentic. We are now more strongly motivated to conjure ideas that align with our personal values and passions. We want not only to create, but to give back or "pay it forward," as Rick says. *Ageless Startup* gives us permission to give ourselves permission to start taking chances again. And all it asks is that we just begin.

Remember when you were a kid? Ready . . . set . . .

INTRODUCTION

To borrow a phrase from AARP's Purpose Prize, "Making a difference is ageless."

Who is an "ageless entrepreneur"? Ageless entrepreneurs fix problems. They are people in the second half of life who use their experience, wisdom, and networks to work from a core purpose, build solutions, and create organizations that help people, enhance their communities, and strengthen themselves. Ageless entrepreneurs make life better. Being an ageless entrepreneur is a way of life.

According to Dr. Carl Schramm, former president of the Kauffman Foundation for Entrepreneurship (a leading organization in entrepreneurship research) and author of *Burn the Business Plan*

(Simon & Schuster, 2019), entrepreneurs over the age of 55 are creating more new businesses than their younger counterparts in the under-35 age group. And it's no surprise why the Boomer generation has a collective wealth of experience, stable retirement income, and transferrable skillsets that make them perfect candidates for the entrepreneurial journey. Schramm also reports that the rate of success for businesses increases with their founders' age. Boomer's businesses have up to five times the success rate of businesses started by Millennials or Gen Zers. Clearly, this cohort of ageless entrepreneurs are busy building startups that stand the test of time—ageless startups.

Research backs the idea that there has never been a better time for ageless entrepreneurs to start their own businesses. In fact, older entrepreneurs are the fastest growing segment of the startup world. According to the 2017 Kauffman Index of Entrepreneurship, the number of startups by younger people has dropped significantly since 1996. There is not an uptick in the percent of new entrepreneurs in the last 20 years until you get to those people 45 and above. The rock stars? Entrepreneurs aged 55 to 64 increased as a percent of total startups from 15 percent of the new entrepreneurs to 25 percent between 1996 and 2016.

You can join this revolution. This is the renaissance age of entrepreneurship, and it's just beginning. The world needs you. Your community needs you. It's time for you to contribute. There has never been a better time to launch your own small venture. You can pursue your own goals and grow your income while changing your community and possibly the world. The time to share your skills and begin building the income you need is here.

Start small.

Start smart.

Start. Right. Now.

That's what I hope you do after you read this book. I write this mostly for my friends in the second half of our lives, the ageless entrepreneurs who want to build ageless startups (though there are insights for everyone interested in starting a new venture). You and I both have knowledge, experience, and networks lacking in younger entrepreneurs. We can use what we've learned over a lifetime to start valuable new enterprises of our own.

There are plenty of problems to fix. If you can't find one, you're not looking hard enough. There are not enough people in the workforce in general. Organizations large and small, for-profit and nonprofit, all need our help to bridge the knowledge gaps and human capital challenges of a changing business landscape that is increasingly dominated by a gig economy mindset.

And to do that, you need to know how to maximize the skillset you bring to the table as a veteran of the workforce, including networking. Entrepreneurship is a game of networks. You need to act in concert with others. Your knowledge and networks are your intellectual property, your greatest strength. Remember the saying: "networking is one letter away from 'not working.'" This book will help you build smart networks to help take your ageless startup to the next level.

You don't need profound insight to start. You don't need to change the world (though you well may). You need to act. You are the driver of what comes next. Which path will you take?

If you need to chase the startup myths of fame, fortune, and adulation, maybe you shouldn't be reading this book. I can't help with those things. But if you're brave enough to consider taking actionable steps that can bring you more independence, increased income, and a chance to help people, then go ahead and give yourself permission to put your ideas into practice.

If you accept the premise of this book—that you should launch your own small enterprise—welcome to your life's next chapter as an ageless entrepreneur.

THE EVIDENCE IS ALL AROUND YOU

The cofounder of Starbucks didn't open his first coffee shop until he was 51. The founders of McDonald's, Coca-Cola, and Kentucky Fried Chicken were all over the age of 50 when they established their businesses.

That's just a snapshot of ageless entrepreneurs in the second half of their lives who have built new organizations to support ideas and causes they were passionate about. Some of those companies were designed to serve their lives only as solopreneurs. Others are growing into national and global businesses designed to employ many. Some are small businesses tailored to help their founders pursue work they love, while others are enterprises positioned to change the world, sometimes by solving small problems one at a time in improbable, difficult locations at home and abroad. Still others are becoming new platforms to help inform and educate people about valuable subjects they love. Most of these ageless entrepreneurs are taking skills, knowledge, and know-how they have built up over the first half of their lives to reach out and serve others in their second half of life.

Many ageless entrepreneurs are following long-suppressed passions they have nurtured for years. Many are looking for better alternatives to sub-par options in the new economy. No matter what entices you about founding and growing an ageless startup, the spirit of entrepreneurship likely guides your path. Entrepreneurship, as I'm covering it in this book applies to most kinds of enterprises including for-profits and nonprofits, slow-growth and fast-growth enterprises. For the most part, the approach I recommend is to avoid raising outside money and pursue self-funding your new enterprise as much as you are able. Go slow, plan carefully, and launch with the attitude of the professional you are.

In this book, you'll meet a diverse array of entrepreneurs with wildly different kinds of experience. You'll meet Dreena Dixon, founder of Chiku Awali African Dance, Arts and Culture, who began her career as a probation officer and rose to the rank of superintendent of a major correctional institution before turning to entrepreneurship. You'll meet Martha Davis Kipcak, who launched an award-winning cheese company and then moved on to food consulting for others. You'll meet Dr. Murelle Harrison, who left academia to tackle a tough organizing and economic development role in Louisiana. Bonnie Addario was at the peak of her career when she was diagnosed with lung cancer at age 56. Bonnie cofounded and chairs a nonprofit whose mission is to raise awareness and funds focused on lung cancer research, and it has raised many millions. You'll read about Haywood Fennell, Sr., a Vietnam War vet, who struggled through homelessness and addiction to find that his passion for writing could lead him to change lives of people in similar circumstances. You'll learn how Joan Beverley Izzo slowly worked on her passion for preserving heirloom family linens into treasured new family keepsakes and how she leveraged her niche to have customers waiting in line to buy products from her ageless startup.

MY AGELESS STARTUP STORY

I wrote this book after decades of working successfully as an independent entrepreneur. My first startup was a small graphics business I launched with a handful of change on my dresser while I was still in college. I didn't know any of the "rules" I was supposed to know. I knew that I had customer demand and the ability to fill it. That business, Banner Graphics, blossomed over time and supported my family for 25 years before I sold it and moved on. I built this small enterprise into a company that had repeat customers on five continents, including many Fortune 500 clients. It was still operating successfully when it hit its 40-year anniversary.

I have found that my life as an innovator blossomed into the most rewarding professional experiences of my life after my 45th birthday.

In the second half of my life, I have been able to launch new businesses and nonprofits using lessons, experiences, and connections that aren't typically available to younger people establishing their careers. As an older entrepreneur, I have been able to apply my knowledge and networks to innovate in both the for-profit and nonprofit sectors, winning significant recognition for both.

As an experienced entrepreneur, I was able to approach problems with a new perspective. With no prior experience in intellectual property, I was able to invent multiple new processes for environmental remediation, receiving nine U.S. and foreign patents along the way. My work was recognized by *Fast Company* as one of the Fast 50, now called the World's 50 Most Innovative Companies. That company, Universal Separators/SmartSkim, is among the smallest businesses to ever win this award. This work also led to one of my inventions being named United States Small Business New Product of the Year by the National Society of Professional Engineers.

In my current role, I helped cofound and lead one of the most innovative regional food development initiatives in the country, Food21 (www.food21.org). I was drawn to this startup by the desire to collaborate with world-class leaders to create new solutions to longstanding problems in the food sector. The mission of Food21 is to expand the breadth and depth of the regional and agricultural economy through market-driven solutions. This is a unique private and public collaboration I helped design and grow. From our base in the Pittsburgh region, I now support artisan food and beverage entrepreneurs across the country with a focus on business development and growth.

As an entrepreneur and innovator in the second half of life, I now have the freedom and the know-how to move between the for-profit and nonprofit worlds to develop innovative solutions where they are needed most.

My story is one that can be replicated by most people in the second half of life. With the right motivation, a passion for helping, and appropriate planning and execution, anyone can do it. It's not hard. It's just new.

WHAT TO EXPECT IN THIS BOOK

As people in the second half of life, we have skills and industry knowledge that can't be taught. This book is designed to give you the tools to apply that know-how to launching your own new small enterprise. This book is designed to help you:

- ▶ Make a smooth transition from working for someone else to working for yourself
- ▶ Minimize your risk and maximize your value
- ▶ Set a pace that's right for you and your business
- ▶ Find the customers who will keep coming back
- ▶ Create a business system that keeps you on track
- ▶ Build your exit strategy into your launch
- ▶ Tackle obstacles with an open mind

Sharing this work is important to me. I've walked the pathway that many people in the second half of life only wonder about. I know where many of the opportunities and dangers are. In this book, I have used that experience to build you a compelling route from wonder to action steps, informing that journey with ideas and examples from my own life, as well as inspiring stories from other older entrepreneurs along the way.

I want you to be able to give yourself ways to explore entrepreneurship in the second half of life. There are many options and paths you can follow that can be built to match your own goals. I want to help you plan your new enterprise effectively and then build a business practice that serves your own needs and helps build better solutions for the world you love.

My approach is different from most startup books. I want you to go slow. This is not a sprint, and you should work at your own pace. Think carefully about what you need so you can craft the best ways to get there using a deliberate strategy for exploring entrepreneurship on your own terms.

I also want to share with people considering this path that planning, launching, and growing a small enterprise of your own is not especially hard, given appropriate initial expectations. Much of it may be new, however, if you're like most people our age who may come from a traditional corporate background. I want you to expect to face new ideas and terms, but most of all, new approaches to how you live your life. All of this is not hard. It's just new.

You will also find inspiring stories told by some of the world's most interesting entrepreneurs who just happen to be in the second half of life. Their ideas and advice will serve to help you recognize your own strengths and suggest ways to build those into your own enterprise.

Are you an ageless entrepreneur ready to build an ageless startup? Let's find out.

WHY START YOUR JOURNEY NOW?

I was poking around the Air and Space Museum at the Smithsonian a few years ago and got stopped cold by a Robert Goddard quote posted in the building. It was from a letter he'd written to H.G. Wells, dated April 20, 1932. I wrote it on a paper scrap that's been posted over my desk ever since. It reads:

> There can be no thought of finishing, for aiming at the stars, both literally and figuratively, is a problem to occupy generations, so that no matter how much progress one makes, there is always the thrill of just beginning.

I really love that: The thrill of just beginning.

Robert Goddard ushered in the space age before that idea even existed outside of science fiction. He was a physicist and inventor who launched the first successful rocket in 1926. During his life, he received little support or recognition. He was also a very private person who lived his life with the aftereffects of tuberculosis. Goddard's work made space flight and exploration possible through his imagination, vision, and leadership. NASA's Goddard Flight Center is named in his honor.

Goddard didn't know where his work would go. Early on, it clearly didn't go the way he'd hoped, even though he was doing great work. His early papers were often sensationalized to the point of misrepresentation and ridicule.

He just persevered. Robert Goddard changed the world, one day at a time.

As you start or grow your enterprise, it will surely not be what you expect. Remember Goddard. Remember that after years of struggle and effort, the thing that he measured his life by was not the rough personal trials and not the global awards. It was the thrill of just beginning.

In all the new enterprises I've launched, there has always been a sense that the full impact of what I was proposing was going to be too big for me to fathom. This can hold you back, or it can motivate you. You don't need to know the final results. You *do* need to relish and remember the excitement of launching.

Don't wait. Your new enterprise is out there to start and grow. What's in it for you? Maybe nothing. Maybe something. Maybe the stars.

However, I guarantee this. Put it in the bank. Forever, you will always have the thrill of just beginning.

All that said, you may be asking, *Isn't this a crazy idea at my age?*

That's something you may be saying to yourself if you are thinking about starting a business later in life. But is it a crazy idea? Sure, you can launch your own small enterprise, but you'll likely be on your own, swimming against a strong media tide of young, hip startup entrepreneurs, right? Wrong.

You are not alone. The Kauffman Foundation for Entrepreneurship keeps a running tally of U.S. startups called their Index of Entrepreneurial Activity. A 2016 index showed that there are about 550,000 new entrepreneurs every month across the country and growing. Every month. Month in and month out.

Those are just official startups on record. The number of people thinking about it or planning to launch new enterprises are probably multiples of that, filling the funnel with hundreds of thousands, possibly millions of startups per month at some stage of being launched.

For the last decade, roughly 320 people out of every 100,000 U.S. adults (0.32 percent) became entrepreneurs each year. What's surprising is who's doing the starting. It's us—older, ageless entrepreneurs. My peers. Your peers.

According to the most recent Kauffman Index published in September 2019, the changes in composition of new entrepreneurs by age between 1996 and 2018 yield some interesting results:

▶ New entrepreneurs in the age group of 20 to 34 fell from 34.3 percent of all new U.S. entrepreneurs in 1996 to 25 percent in 2018.

▶ New entrepreneurs in the age group of 35 to 44 fell from 27.4 percent of all new U.S. entrepreneurs in 1996 to 24 percent in 2018.

Where do ageless entrepreneurs fit in the story? New entrepreneurs in the age group of 45 to 54 rose from 23.5 percent of all new U.S. entrepreneurs in 1996 to 25.3 percent in 2018. And, amazingly, new entrepreneurs in the age group of 55 to 64 rose from 14.8 percent of all new U.S. entrepreneurs in 1996 to 25.8 percent in 2018. If you add the new entrepreneurs in the 45 to 54 range (26.13 percent) with entrepreneurs in the 55 to 64 range (25.46 percent) you get a total of 51.1 percent of all U.S. startups led by people over the age of 45.

Taking the total number of U.S. startups per month (550,000) and multiplying that by the percent of senior startups on record, you get startling results: 281,050 startups per month are led by people 45 and older. That amounts to a total of 3,372,600 U.S. startups per year led by senior entrepreneurs.

All of this data points to the fact that entrepreneurship is alive and well, especially in the over-45 demographic. So, no, you are not alone.

The over-45 demographic is primed for entrepreneurial success. Why? For one thing, we're living longer. We have extensive knowledge and networks to call on as resources. The tools and techniques for spreading the word to potential customers worldwide have never been more accessible, and the costs of using them have never been lower. The second half of life might be the perfect time to start a new enterprise that matches your goals and circumstances.

What this means for you is that you can become an entrepreneur at any point in your life. Age is an advantage. Wisdom is a resource. Your networks of contacts are the basis for a smart new enterprise you can call your own. There is plenty of help, and plenty of peers are available—but the key is to be proactive and make the moves to connect with those resources. You don't have to wait for magic to happen to transform your life. In this chapter, I'll lay the groundwork for getting started by determining your

Ageless Entrepreneur Spotlight

Michael L. Smolens, founder/chairman/CEO, collector of puzzle pieces, DotSub, and 2011 Purpose Prize Fellow (New York)

Q: *How did you find your current "encore" career?*

A: Even today at age 70, I am starting some major new businesses all over the world, and there is nothing encore about them. If you love what you do, the word retirement does not exist, as retirement is doing what you want to do each morning when you get up, and I have done that my whole life.

Q: *Are there any mistakes you can share from your own encore career?*

A: If I had to think of adding something, it would have been to get a mentor early on.

Q: *What is the best advice you would share with someone in the second half of life considering entrepreneurship?*

A: Spend all your time finding your passion, and then go for it—it will happen.

"why" and identifying a roadmap for your ageless startup journey that is comprised of three parts: permission, planning, and practice. Then, we'll dive into why the best time is right now to discover your niche and join the renaissance age of entrepreneurship.

IDENTIFY YOUR "WHY"

Why do people start businesses in their second half of life? Money is certainly a contributing factor as to why people start new enterprises, but it is rarely the main driver. Sustainability and longevity for your ageless startup are vitally important, and if your new enterprise is not paying for itself, it won't survive. It's not sustainable if it's not repeatable and, thus, not profitable for the long term. But beyond that, the "why" question is the far more interesting one.

Many people in the second half of life want to make a contribution back to their communities and their world. They want to pay it forward, to take the knowledge and skills they have developed with the support of others and make a difference in the lives of others, to serve the industries they know and love, as well as to help grow the communities they live in or the communities of interest they share with others around the world. Others have an extensive skillset (often cultivated in a leadership role) that they want to not only use, but monetize for the next phase in their professional life. Perhaps they have the skills and know-how, but aren't sure how to make it a business. Or perhaps they have the spark of an idea borne of years in the corporate trenches that they are ready to create a startup around.

What about you? What is your reason for wanting to start a business now? If you were to write down a list of "why" questions that helped you define your interest in launching an ageless startup, what would you include? My personal list would include:

- Why am I ready to learn about new opportunities as an entrepreneur?
- Why are my current circumstances not sufficient to support the dreams I want to pursue?
- Why am I capable of doing more? What do I know? Who can I call on to help?

> ▶ Why is this time right for me to consider entrepreneurship as a solution?
> ▶ Why will the ideas I'm considering help me? Help my community?

These are the questions that drive me when I'm looking at a new problem. Yours will be different, but the common thread is to identify the mission you want to accomplish, how you can infuse your own values to create a new solution, and what goals you will set to measure the project.

You can do this. Dive deeper into the skills you already have. Develop them further. Grow your networks. Reach out and look for help, mentors, tools, and advice. These are the factors you must consider first. Money comes after that.

It is indeed the renaissance age of entrepreneurship. And it's just beginning. Give yourself permission to act, then step forward. Your capacity to make a difference increases as you grow older. Why start now? You have knowledge and networks that matter.

ENVISION YOUR STARTUP JOURNEY

Starting a business is not a singular event, but a journey. Specifically, it's a journey with three important phases: permission, planning, and practice. Let's walk through each one.

Permission

Most people who have not worked as entrepreneurs may be scared off by the myths, jargon, and hype that accompany the subject. They will talk about it. They may go to seminars or watch motivational videos online. They will dance around the subject for so long that they accumulate enough reasons to put off launching their own enterprise until they are not able to.

In my years of counseling entrepreneurs, I've found that the biggest hurdle to joining the startup movement is not the business planning or even the funding issues. Imposter syndrome does not discriminate, and sometimes the biggest hurdle to entrepreneurship is that people won't give themselves permission to try.

If you keep your aspirations realistic, the only permission you need is your own.

Giving yourself permission to try, perhaps even to fail at some or all of it, is the critical key to taking any next steps. Giving yourself permission to start small, to start slow, and to start with your own needs and values firmly established is what *Ageless Startup* is all about.

As an ageless entrepreneur, you may feel a greater sense of self-empowerment. After all, you've worked for the first half of your lifetime—most likely for someone else. So, giving yourself permission to be your own boss may be easier than you think. Older entrepreneurs have a unique perspective. We have typically tried more things. We've developed valuable lists of "what not to do next time." We know the kinds of people who can be trusted to share our entrepreneurial vision and those who can't. We typically don't need to develop instant cash flows from our enterprises (at least, if we are starting with some money already saved or invested). We are more interested in solving problems than building our resumes. Why wouldn't you allow yourself to create something that's for YOU and no one else?

You aren't an island, though. When you start to consider your new enterprise, make sure to discuss the implications with your own family first. They need reassurance that you have clear boundaries about the amount of money you intend to commit to the project and the amount of time you're willing to spend. Both your family and your intended customers want to see a clear purpose in what you are offering and how you intend to deliver that benefit.

There are new generations of people emerging and even newer histories to write for yourself, your family, and the world. You've earned the wisdom you have. No matter what subject your expertise may be in, no matter how obscure it may seem to you right now, in a world of more than seven and a half billion people, there are communities of people that need you, starting with your own. Take the time to explain this to your family and get their buy-in before you proceed.

The trick is to join the conversation, then act. But I can't give you permission to be an entrepreneur. Only you can give yourself that permission.

Take a deep breath. Pause. Exhale.

Take another moment. Keep breathing. I'll wait.

Permission granted? OK, now I can help.

Planning

Once you've given yourself permission to pursue an ageless startup, do a little blue-sky planning that briefly lays out your goals and expectations. (Chapter 5 will give you a deeper dive into creating your final business plan.)

The joy of planning for older entrepreneurs is that you don't have to lay out a fantasy growth scenario for attracting investors and taking your company public. If you want that kind of business, you'll need to expand your research significantly. The vast majority of us will create business plans that support us individually as solo entrepreneurs. The U.S. Census Bureau defines this kind of businesses as something called *nonemployer businesses.*

If you think this is some small, neglected part of the U.S. economy, think again. Over three quarters of ALL businesses in the U.S. are nonemployer businesses. That's just under 25 million solo entrepreneurs out of a total of about 32 million U.S. businesses.

You can plan this for yourself. It's not hard. It's just new. You can plan an enterprise that meets your own needs and expectations. The plan you create for yourself does not have to buy into the myth of the sleep-deprived, fully consumed entrepreneur sleeping under their desk to get a jump on tomorrow.

You can set up your ageless startup to match your own schedule and your own interests and abilities. About 50 percent of nonemployer business owners spend less than 20 hours a week working for or managing their business. About 20 percent spend between 20 and 40 hours. Only 30 percent of nonemployer businesses spend at least 40 hours a week on the business.

You will have to realistically consider how much income you want your new enterprise to produce. This is where planning to go slow initially helps. If you can create a plan that does not generate a lot of income initially, you will be setting your expectations appropriately, as almost everything takes longer than you want when starting a new business. That said, on average, nonemployer businesses earn about $47,000 annually. That's revenue, not profit. Your results will vary.

I tell friends to plan their ageless startups around making a contribution to their communities doing something they love. Communities can be their physical surroundings or a business community of interests that spans the globe.

Plan to charge appropriately for your services at a rate that exceeds what you will spend. How much you grow your enterprise, and how smartly you hold to—and improve on—your plan will determine how much income you generate for yourself.

Planning is not a mystical process of divining the future. Planning is an exercise in looking into yourself to determine what you think is worth pursuing and then telling yourself the story of how you will get there. As you consider starting your own enterprise, the stories you believe will strongly influence your outcome. Ignore shortcuts and fast answers. Your plan—your way forward—is your story to write.

Practice

I like thinking about new and emerging enterprises as practices.

Think of orthopedic practices or law practices, or tax, accounting, or consulting practices among many other professional examples. All of these share something in common with a new startup—they are deeply rooted in the day-to-day practice of using your unique skill set. As a startup or emerging business, you will benefit in this new economy by holding yourself to this level of professionalism, no matter what kind of enterprise you're involved in.

Professionals who operate their businesses continually practice. They get better. They innovate. They continue to grow. They continue to find new ways to add value for their customers.

Or they fail.

What is also implied is that you must plan strategies and business processes that make you increasingly proficient in the professional practice you are creating. It is vital that you learn, capture, and improve with every transaction. Building a successful practice in any field means establishing a professional business model as well as a subject expertise.

You can enter any part of our economy at a small scale that matches your goals and aspirations. It is crucial that you build a professional practice and that you personally grow in professionalism as you develop your business model. Treat your business like the professional practice it is right from the start.

Ageless Entrepreneur Spotlight

Wickham Boyle, cofounder of Just Shea and 2015 AARP Purpose Prize Fellow
(New York)

Q: *What did you do as your first career?*

A: I guess changing careers has never been terrifying to me. So, at 60-ish when I couldn't find any good full-time work, I decided to volunteer for projects that looked just marvelous and where I might contribute. I was consulting at an organization that helps women become thought leaders, and there was a young woman who had a notion to begin a project in Ghana. I always had a passion for Africa, and so I leapt in.

Q: *What would you do differently now that you've had some time developing your current adventure?*

A: Well, I am on to designing and envisioning a next adventure. We have morphed JUST SHEA into local administration. But I believe we could have articulated that as a goal earlier in the process, instead of being seen as owners or the boss of a company in Africa rather, perhaps a catalyst.

Q: *Are there any mistakes you can share from your own current career?*

A: Write everything down. Send constant email missives saying, "Here is what I think we agreed to." Or, "What do you think?"

Q: *What is the best piece of advice you would share with someone in the second half of life considering entrepreneurship?*

A: Be open. Don't have a preconceived notion of what might work or where your skills can fit. Be expansive and hopeful.

FIND YOUR NICHE

If you find yourself needing or wanting to work beyond typical retirement age, you are not alone. While direct employment still plays a predominant role in life after official retirement, self-employment is growing as a preferred option. People in the second half of life are deferring retirement and opting for entrepreneurship and continued employment to fulfill personal and financial goals. As a cohort, those of us in the over-50 age group are voting with our actions. Record numbers of small businesses are being launched by ageless entrepreneurs.

The good news is that there are opportunities for creating new small-scale but highly professional practices in every niche in the economy. Most of us will follow the solo entrepreneur/nonemployer business model (which you first read about earlier in this chapter). According to the U.S. Small Business Administration (SBA), the range of industries represented by nonemployer businesses and startups is vast enough to cover 80 percent of known industry subsectors. These include solo gigs in fields like entertainment and rideshare services as well as small stores, administrative services, consulting, pet care, dating services, real estate, data processing, small-scale manufacturing, and much more.

A nonemployer business doesn't generate any paychecks (not even to you, the owner). You as the owner are not guaranteed anything. You are able to remove money appropriately, from the business to you, as funds become available. In my world, this is called running businesses where you eat what you kill.

Using self-employment and entrepreneurship to bridge the time between paid employment and retirement is on the rise. It gives older entrepreneurs more control over their time and more opportunities to explore and develop their passions—in other words, an ageless startup is perfect for monetizing your niche.

I have seen this prove true in my own journey. I began this "bridging" process in my mid-40s and took my first steps toward ageless entrepreneurship without knowing I was part of a trend.

I started a small T-shirt printing business while in college in the early 1970s. I funded it from a loose change jar on a dresser in my college dorm. After college, I worked doing business development for a couple of startups, but I kept the graphics enterprise alive. When one of those companies tried to take advantage of me, I told them I wasn't interested in being screwed and was returning to my graphics business. There was precious little "there" there at my tiny little enterprise, but the business was in place and served its purpose as a bridge to what came next.

My wife and I grew that graphics business and raised our family. What started with a need to escape a bad job grew into to a beloved family enterprise over the next 25 years. We were able to raise our kids in the business and bring them to adulthood in an entrepreneurial environment. Our graphics business grew from a loose change jar into a family-supporting small business with customers on five continents.

When we did sell the business in the mid-1990s, it was clear that computers would be able to replicate most of the artisan-scale craftsmanship we had used to grow our business. It seemed like a great time to create a bridge to the next business. I sold Banner Graphics to one of our best vendors. They knew our ethics and our values, and we had an honorable history of commercial transactions between us.

When I last met with the folks we sold it to, the business was still going strong 15 years after the sale—making it a 40-year entrepreneurship success story that started with loose change. We found our niche and innovated continuously to offer new solutions in the graphic industry. We solved problems. We stayed true to our mission.

The best part of this kind of entrepreneurship is that most everyone wants to see you succeed. Your new enterprise is not taking a slice from another person's pie. You're baking a new pie.

FOCUS ON YOUR PASSION, WISDOM, AND NETWORK

I was 45 years old when we sold Banner Graphics. I had just cut ties with my 25-year-old career. It was a profoundly scary, yet exhilarating, time. What emerged has been the best story of my life. I became an ageless entrepreneur and turned the second half of my life into a platform for finding my niche by following my passions. We used the small amount of money from that sale to bridge our way to the next business, one that had been slowly percolating for many years.

As a young person, I had learned some entry-level skills about water treatment from my father. In the subsequent years, that industry had become much more sophisticated, but I knew there was still a strong need for some of the solutions I'd helped my dad develop. Over the next 20 years, I worked as an entrepreneur in several fields, both for-profit and nonprofit. The most important lessons I learned from that decision to sell my business and move into a mode of ageless entrepreneurship was how to use entrepreneurship to take smart, slow, and calculated leaps into the second half of life.

Startups created by senior entrepreneurs are changing the world of work. Senior entrepreneurs bring three important elements to the table:

1. Passion
2. Wisdom
3. Deep networks

These are the kinds of startups that can provide solutions that help communities grow wisely and securely into the future.

As we get older, most of us find that we begin to focus on the passions that motivate our lives. When applied to startups, there is no stronger force than focused passion. Ageless entrepreneurs are driven to make a difference and to reach into themselves to express those passions through their work. No other motivating force can equal it.

The wisdom and deep networks we carry into our startups are assets that are impossible to quantify but critical to the success of the mission. Wisdom in this sense is not described by academic degrees but by a person's know-how. We bring experience from a wide array of fields, no matter who we are. We have navigated work and community to come to a time in life where we can apply that know-how to solving problems that others don't have solutions for. Our deep networks are made up of the web of friends, colleagues, family, and friends of friends that make up the wide-ranging knowledge framework we can call on to help when needed.

Tying your passions, wisdom, and networks together is the best way possible to take on new challenges and build success into your new enterprise. These are the startups that are most resilient. These built-in advantages will help you grow through all the inevitable ups and downs startups face. Together, they also constitute the strongest advantage that ageless entrepreneurs have in the marketplace.

FOLLOW PEERS WITH PURPOSE

The *Purpose Prize* recognizes people over 50 who are combining their passion and experience for social good. Paul Tasner is a *Purpose Prize* Fellow, who started his new business at the age of 66. He is using his skills, insight, and experience to build a new business.

In a recent TED Talk, Paul talked about his experience and he summed up the process nicely: "I am doing the most rewarding and meaningful work of my life right now." What Paul said he needed most when he launched his new venture was not financing or technical support. There are plenty of those resources out there. What Paul said was missing was the ability to interact with other older entrepreneurs. He told his TED audience, "I had no role models, absolutely none. That twentysomething app developer from Silicon Valley was NOT my role model."

If you search the news for entrepreneurship stories, there is an overwhelming amount of information about the camaraderie of young entrepreneurs bonding over all-nighters and market disruption. Our culture celebrates young entrepreneurs (as we should), but we ignore older entrepreneurs at our peril. In times of great flux and change, there is great merit in first-hand experience. People with experience represent knowledge, networks, and creative solutions waiting to be developed.

If you are an older entrepreneur, don't look to the news to find peer entrepreneurs. The media is after disruptive twenty- and thirtysomethings. If you want peers, look in your own field. Look to your professional and personal networks. Reach out to them. Follow them on social media and recommend them when you are able. We need to build our own peer networks, and it starts by supporting one another. Think of your entrepreneurial life as a rope. The more individual strands you can weave in, the stronger the rope grows. You don't know when you will need each strand, but the power of the whole will deliver a lifeline as your ageless startup grows.

For example, when thinking about starting my own small business, especially as an older entrepreneur, I wondered just what it was I could contribute to my peer network and what, in turn, I could learn from them. I asked myself:

▶ What did I have to offer that made me special?

▶ Could my own experiences still matter?

▶ Do the years of experience of my peers still matter?

▶ How much experience and wisdom could that add up to?

As many of us in this age range look to develop new opportunities to grow personally and professionally, we look for resources that can support our goals. If there are 100 million seniors, each with an average of 30 years of work experience, that translates into 3 billion years of knowledge. In this enormous number are unlimited solutions, countless new startups, and the potential to make the planet a much better place.

We don't need the drama of competing in markets where corporations demand outsized shareholder returns. We need the satisfaction that we've helped make the campground a little better for the next group.

Look to your older peers. Develop professional networks within this group that you can tap when needed. You can connect with plenty of knowledge and experience as our cohort of older workers emerge as entrepreneurs.

The most powerful tool for solving problems is a knowledge network—one made up of subject-matter experts upon whom you can rely for information (not necessarily traditional networking). You are plugged into many of these already, and reaching out will grow those connections and the value they contain.

I work to make connections to ideas and new projects all day long. Many never stick. Some end up being dumb. Others still don't resurface for a year or more. You never know until you get in the game and make connections with interesting people and ideas.

There is a great vibrancy in experience. Ideas and the minds that create them are gems to be polished. Celebrate them. Honor them. Most of all, put them to work. Here are some ways you can maximize your knowledge and resource base:

▶ Keep your networks vibrant. Check in with colleagues, and ask if they need help with no expectation of returns.

▶ Don't be afraid to consider approaching younger people to advise and mentor you. Learning can be an intergenerational exercise.

▶ When you meet someone interesting in the media or in your industry, follow up. Reach out on LinkedIn or directly. Don't waste an opportunity to grow by letting potentially interesting new relationships go fallow.

▶ Introduce your startup to all the public agencies and forums you think could be valuable. Ask for their help. Participate in their public forums. Make contributions without expecting immediate returns. Some of the agencies you can look to include:
  – Small business development centers (SBDCs)
  – Tech school, college, and university entrepreneurship centers
  – Economic development agencies

 Ageless Entrepreneur Spotlight

Martha Davis Kipcak, founder of Mighty Fine Food (Wisconsin)

Q: *Are there any mistakes you can share from your own current career?*

A: Every day should be an opportunity to discover and grow and correct whatever didn't work before. There were definitely disappointments and gut punches and states of bewilderment. But I chose to see them more as obstacles to overcome rather than mistakes.

Q: *What is the best piece of advice you would share with someone in the second half of life considering entrepreneurship?*

A: Own your shit. Nothing is as exhausting as people who refuse to own any error—intentional or accidental. Own your shit. People will respect you for it. And you can respect yourself. Work every day to maintain good emotional, spiritual and physical health. Cultivate curiosity and tenacity and wonder.

Listen more. Talk less.

Stay active and engaged in people, in ideas, in what truly brings value to life.

- Local chambers of commerce
- State agencies focused on business development and entrepreneurship
- Local peer-to-peer business networks

There are many points of entry to find help and support for starting your new enterprise. Be modest in your expectations. Ask for help respectfully, and you will get respect back.

START SLOW

Doesn't creating new enterprises mean that everything happens quickly and with great difficulty? Aren't new enterprises built around hard choices, hard work, and endless hours? That's a myth, and you don't have to buy into it if you want to be successful.

Consider the word *hard*. The word often implies something onerous and difficult. Something that we think is hard is something we typically don't want to do. If something is new to us, it is usually something we don't know how to do.

Now, let's put that in context. A new enterprise should be something you want to do. You've been doing new things most of your life, so you can put your skill set to work to help overcome the hard/new challenges. If your new enterprise is something you *want* to do, the hardness will fall away as you learn more.

That said, how do you rectify the need to learn with the typical rush of scaling a startup? Those stories of manic young entrepreneurs sprinting to stay ahead of their own predictions, investors, and cash flow meltdowns are great for TV. This is often referred to as "building the airplane in-flight." But there are far smarter startup paths available, especially suited to ageless entrepreneur launches—the slow startup is one such path.

Slow startups are new organizations that are typically self-funded and that do not need to meet rapid financial goals. They are enterprises designed by their founders to meet those founders' personal goals and aspirations for success. Certainly, there is a need for consistent revenue for the entity to be sustainable, but slow startups can be created, planned, and executed in ways that develop slowly over time to match a founder's resources and available time.

One benefit of slow startups is that you can bring your knowledge and skills to community problems at your own pace. You can help others fighting problems you are passionate about by bringing your new startup to their fight. However, if you are rushing to market, it may be harder to focus on community-based, long-term solutions.

How do slow startups affect their intended markets? These organizations benefit the greater goals of the communities they serve as well as the goals of the entrepreneur in several ways. By starting slow, ageless entrepreneurs can:

- Serve both their founders and their target markets without a rush to meet rapid revenue targets
- Revitalize their communities and their industries by offering new ways to think about how change happens and causing that change at the pace that best serves the entrepreneur
- Model new ways of building unexpected business and community networks to solve problems
- Show their peers and our communities just what inspired, vibrant problem-solving looks like and the kind of quality results that come from new approaches
- Inform and educate communities about issues they are passionate about

These kinds of contributions require the opposite of rushing. They require that the entrepreneur be prepared with sustainable solutions and, more importantly, to have taken the time to understand the problems being addressed and the impact their new enterprise can have on those who are already in the fray.

If you approach your new startup as a marathon, not a sprint, you can put in place the ideas and attitudes which will help you succeed in the long run. Ignore the rush-to-market hype. Ignore the cultural myths that imply entrepreneurship is only for the fastest gazelles among us. This is your life. This is your contribution. You can give birth to your enterprise at your speed. You can grow it on your timetable with the time you have available.

If you live by someone else's clock, you will be accepting other people's definitions of what you should do, not what your own planning and work has inspired you to launch.

Fine-Tune Your Initial Idea

As you start slow, take the time to research what you love as the first step. Let the research take you into challenging new directions, not the same old same old. What's emerging? What's exciting? Ask yourself questions like these:

▶ Where in your own life do you see a need for improvement in the world?

▶ What makes you mad about the way some things are done?

▶ What scares you? It must scare others. How would you fix or mitigate this issue?

▶ In your own work life, what parts of that work are no longer done to the standards you want to see?

▶ Where are labor shortages in your work life most acute?

▶ Where in your own life do you see businesses and organizations cutting corners that negatively affect their operations?

▶ What opportunities are you hearing about from other places that aren't yet represented in your community?

▶ What problems or issues are you passionate about and that you think others would benefit by having access to your information?

▶ Was there an event in your life in which you volunteered for something that lit you up? Can you bring a different perspective to improving those issues?

You can be a thought leader, no matter your age, by supplying effective services to these markets. Learn from all the things that many in the retirement cohort may be inclined to run from: technology, digital tools, and social networks. Embrace it. Take the opportunity to slow down and make changes that utilize the new digital and cultural tools that are appearing. Then hurry up and try them out.

Are you going to get rich with your launch? It happens, but the strongest likelihood is that if you plan it right, you will have a sustainable job for yourself going forward—one that isn't dependent on distant corporate managers or the vagaries of the specific geography where you find yourself.

If you team up to market yourself with like-minded peers of all ages, if you build out the skills you have in collaboration with others in your chosen field, your networks can light the way to new innovations and new business models. It does not take a lot of money to start most new enterprises. It takes the kind of skills and knowledge that most people have but often don't value: time, patience, deep understanding of a specific subject, and the ability to take a longer view. At any age, but especially in the second half of life, take the time to acquire the skills to create your own small enterprise. Done right, it may be the best security you can create for yourself in this economy. More importantly, you can help create a new, better, and more secure economy that benefits everyone in society.

It's not hard; it's just new. So start slow.

JOIN THE RENAISSANCE AGE OF ENTREPRENEURSHIP

Congratulations, you're living in the renaissance age of entrepreneurship.

Look around. New tools, new problem-solving skills, and new worlds of innovation are exploding like fireworks all around us. So are the problems that need fixing. The world needs solutions. If you want to join the fray, there has never been a better time to make a contribution.

We are awash in new potential for entrepreneurial solutions in every facet of our societies, from high science to brickmaking to widget manufacturing to local services. Improbably powerful tools are available for free or at modest cost. The world is searching for innovative solutions to growing numbers of problems.

One place you can find people searching for those innovative solutions is to look on Main Street. Global problems are evident on the local level, and small business owners are stepping up to help solve them. From the need for a better environment or stronger support systems for an aging population to internet accessibility in rural areas and transportation redesign in urban areas, there are all sorts of issues on the local level that need our attention. Lucky for us, entrepreneurship is in a cycle of growth where it boosts success of the local area, which further promotes entrepreneurship on a larger scale.

In a paper written a while back titled "Entrepreneurship and the City," Harvard economist Professor Edward Glaeser identified some great reasons entrepreneurship flourishes in cities. While this research looked specifically at what made cities more successful, I have no doubt that the same findings can be applied to any region and probably any country.

The paper concludes that it is the culture of entrepreneurship that is critical to the success of a city. Specifically, cities don't have entrepreneurial cultures by some stroke of good luck. They succeed because they support and educate the widest number of people who then become entrepreneurs.

Professor Glaeser wrote that, "local entrepreneurship depends mainly on having the right kind of people." And I would suggest that to create the most efficient and widespread effects, the right kind of people would be those who are respected, supported, and trained to learn from failure and to grow in sustainable ways. That's a real culture of innovation.

There is a tantalizing reference in Professor Glaeser's abstract for my ageless entrepreneur friends: "Self-employment is particularly associated with abundant, older citizens and with the presence of input suppliers." Is this a knock on other kinds of enterprise creation? Of course not. Those high tech, biotech, and nanotech models can be wonderful and produce spectacular results. But those models aren't the only viable alternatives. The entire entrepreneurship movement needs support and respect for the whole culture to grow and prosper.

You do the numbers. Every region needs more entrepreneurs and more small enterprises to be successful. That is NOT the same as more headline-grabbing, venture-funded firms. It's sheer numbers. More entrepreneurs and more enterprises make the culture succeed. From this perspective, risk in the economy gets spread around and diversified, more people get to contribute, and more people become engaged in solving problems.

You can energize your life by creating something new and valuable for your community while achieving your own goals and fulfilling long-nurtured dreams. You can join a remarkable revolution.

According to entrepreneurship writer and speaker Elizabeth White, citing the Kauffman Foundation in her book *55, Underemployed, and Faking Normal: Your Guide to a Better Life* (Simon & Schuster, 2019):

▶ One quarter (25.5 percent) of all new entrepreneurs are over 55.
▶ This percent was only 14.8 in 1996.
▶ 92 percent of all businesses in the U.S. are microenterprises, comprising between one and five employees, including the owner.

The renaissance is here for all of us—for Boomers, for young people, and for everyone in between. There is no alchemy involved in starting new enterprises. The opportunities are everywhere, and the tools for executing are cheap or often free.

What you most need is common sense, viable planning, and the stubbornness to keep putting one foot in front of the other every single day.

The magic comes as you watch your new enterprise take its first steps, then build momentum, then take flight. And where will you take your new enterprise? What is the environment you'll be entering? Well, your enterprise will be in good company.

The U.S. Small Business Administration published a report by Daniel Wilmoth in 2016 titled, "The Ascent of the Senior Entrepreneur." The report documents the percentage of people in different age ranges who are self-employed. The percent of individuals who were self-employed rose from 4.2 percent in 1988 to 5.4 percent in 2015. Surprisingly, the percent of individuals under age 62 who were self-employed fell, while the number of those over 62 rose. This tells me that senior entrepreneurship is on a steady rise.

This is partially based on a larger trend of people over 62 being employed at higher rates than in the past. Many of us, seniors, want to keep working and contributing. It may come in part from economic necessity, but it is also largely driven by a need to contribute and to participate. It is from this larger trend that the self-employed group emerges.

This is a time of great change, and one of the ways ageless entrepreneurs can contribute is by connecting the great store of experience and wisdom developed among our peers over the decades and turning that value into new solutions and new businesses.

You are among friends. Senior entrepreneurship is growing rapidly. Put your talents, skills, networks, and passions to work fixing problems in the world.

There has never been more need. There has never been a better time.

THINK LIFE-CHANGING—NOT LIFESTYLE

When politicians, policy makers, and academics discuss entrepreneurship, they typically don't want to talk about self-employment or small businesses that create a few jobs, no matter what they say. Instead, they focus on the big-ticket popularity of entrepreneurship as a panacea for business-as-usual and the "superstar" stories of those who started their own companies and made it big with their brand. People in positions of power (those with steady paychecks) who pontificate about the glories of entrepreneurship are usually not focusing on the vast majority of startups reflected by new businesses that are one-person operations or those that create jobs for a just few people.

In my past life as an economic developer, my peers referred (almost sneeringly) to such small operations as "lifestyle entrepreneurs." In other words, people who merely dabbled in their hobby part-time and considered it a business. These were not the kind of businesses they wanted. They wanted startups that grew rapidly and that employed hundreds or even thousands of people. Those were the "real" startups, not those "lifestyle businesses." It's easy to think like that when you have a paycheck, and you're paid to talk about other people taking risks.

More than three quarters of all businesses in the country are led by solo entrepreneurs (those "nonemployer" businesses I mentioned earlier in this chapter). The U.S. Census Bureau reports that 76.2 percent of all businesses in the U.S. had no paid employees in 2016 (1), the most recent year for which final data is available. More than three quarters of all businesses in the country are led by solo entrepreneurs. When you break out the economy by sectors, an even more interesting picture emerges for those considering entrepreneurship, as seen in Table 1–1 on page 24.

Table 1-1. Solo Entrepreneurship by Sector

U.S. Sector	Percent of Which Are Nonemployer Establishments
Arts, Entertainment, and Recreation	91.0
Transportation and Warehousing	89.0
Educational Services	87.4
Real Estate, Rental, and Leasing	87.3
Administrative Support	83.6
Professional, Scientific, and Technical Services	79.2
Construction	78.0
Information	69.7
Health Care and Social Assistance	68.7
Retail Trade	65.2
Finance and Insurance	60.0
Manufacturing	54.5

(Source = United States Census Bureau (1))

This is not the picture that is typically painted in today's business media. Some forms of solo entrepreneurship are more visible than others. The classic side hustle describes someone doing part-time work in their available free time to earn extra income. These are represented by ridesharing and meal delivery services customers can contract with to provide services. These are valuable entry points into solo entrepreneurship, but they don't tell the full story of the opportunity.

Solopreneurs dominate many industries in the sheer number of establishments. While the total sales revenue coming out of larger firms usually far exceeds the revenue generated by solo entrepreneurs as a sector, the point is clear that there are many opportunities for entrepreneurship across all sectors of the economy. There is very likely a demand for the skills you have developed.

Ageless entrepreneurs (*all* entrepreneurs, really) should push back against this stigmatizing "lifestyle entrepreneur" description. There is no greater outcome than increased control over your own life on terms of your choosing. Your new business does not have to meet pre-defined measures of success that make other people's articles and reporting look better. Those writing the reports aren't in the trenches. They are not creating solutions. They have no skin in the game. They are reading from history—not creating a future.

"Lifestyle entrepreneur" sounds dismissive, as though people are dabbling in business to feed their need for a hobby. If someone tries to belittle your vision with this kind of language, fight back. You and your new business can be every bit as valuable to your community as big businesses—perhaps even more so. For those of us in the trenches, we should change that phrase from "lifestyle" to "life-changing" business.

Life-changing businesses can come in all flavors of entrepreneurship. For ageless startups, the solo entrepreneur providing knowledge-based services is an ideal mode, though not the only one. Solo entrepreneurs have the most control over their own time and are not responsible for managing others. They can buy services from other ageless entrepreneurs when needed rather than taking on the responsibility of employing people. For others who want to simply operate side-hustle enterprises while they continue their day jobs, ageless startups offer a compelling platform. You can operate as your own company, rather than simply as an independent contractor. This way, when you decide to make the leap from paid employment to self-employment, all the business tools will be in place.

SCARE YOURSELF

Nothing should ever be considered "done" in your enterprise life. If it is, so are you.

One thing is always certain: Your first attempts at enterprise certainly won't be your best. I don't care if you're building a nonprofit venture or

Ageless Entrepreneur Spotlight

Glenn Ford, founder of InCity Farms (Minnesota)

Q: *How did you find your current passion?*

A: I grew up as a kid from inner-city Chicago. As I continued to rise through higher-level corporate jobs, it moved me further and further away from the kinds of communities that I was raised in. As I would return on visits to those communities, all I saw was continued decline. I am an example of the kinds of talents that are present in those communities and felt someone needed to reach back and bring people forward. I believe strongly in that issue and needed to create a company so I could address it unencumbered.

Q: *Are there any mistakes you can share from your own current career?*

A: I am unencumbered by mistakes and do not make it a point to tally them as it serves no purpose. Along the way in entrepreneurship, if you are truly reaching for the big win, you will have mini-setbacks. Also, get connected to other entrepreneurs who have the courage to be a business owner. Surround yourself with positive people, and avoid the negative people.

Q: *What is the best piece of advice you would share with someone in the second half of life considering entrepreneurship?*

A: Please jump in; the water is fine, and your contribution is needed. I would also say, do not take small business for granted because you were once a big company executive. While small business may have less revenue than your previous role, it is dramatically different and harder. In entrepreneurship, you have to create the momentum in a company and be able to fend off reputations created in the decades of work that came before you.

I would add that entrepreneurship is wonderful when your aspirations for it are also in service to others and not simply a get-rich scheme. Get over the common thoughts that you are no longer working for someone else. There will always be someone you need to answer to, so move forward, recognizing that what you do matters a great deal and that you are in service to others. Get this correct, and the business will reward you greatly.

launching your own service business. Startups can be scary from a zillion directions, but one of the biggest is admitting that you might screw it up.

Fear is good, sometimes, and it can work in your favor. Economic value and sustainability come from information, experience, and judgement. Give yourself permission to try and to fail, then try again.

Fail in small ways again, and again, and again. Look carefully for what it teaches you. Search out the wisdom of setbacks as much or even more than the victories. You can only become sustainable by knowing what doesn't work.

Starting up new companies and starting up new products is a very uncertain business. You typically don't have much of anything for reference. Everything around you is new, something-from-nothing stuff. But there is a reason to be drawn toward uncertainty: That's where the problems live. That's where the need is.

If you can learn to live with some level of uncertainty, you can find your contribution. Uncertainty teaches you to create new ways to tackle real problems.

If older—ageless—entrepreneurs are to succeed, what kind of inputs do they need to focus on? What could help make your enterprise succeed?

Think about those questions then go "scare" yourself. Get in the weeds a bit. Give yourself the permission to fail, to learn, and to keep going. The more you fail, the more you learn—and the more you contribute to a culture of entrepreneurial innovation.

FIND THE OPPORTUNITIES HIDDEN IN PLAIN SIGHT

When planning your startup or growing your enterprise, you've got to first decide who your customers are and what value you can bring to them. Where are those potential customers hiding? What are your best market opportunities?

When you are trying to clear a path for your product or service, it looks pretty daunting. In fact, it may look downright chaotic. You can look at a million details so hard and for so long that the trees disappear. You can be left with only a forest of details and nothing to act on.

Good. That kind of confusion dissuades people without a plan. But as an ageless entrepreneur, you've seen things—a lot of things—in your professional life. And you know that sometimes, the best opportunities for a business can be found in the chaos. Sometimes, those opportunities are hidden in plain sight.

One of my favorite books and fount of advice is *The Long Tail* (Hachette Books, 2008) by Chris Anderson, former editor-in-chief of *Wired* magazine. My summary will be too short, but the basic idea behind the concept of long tails is that carefully searched and sorted, patterns can be pulled from chaos. Anderson posits that, culturally and economically, we are moving away from a business environment in which there are a few huge players (whether that be companies, products, or trends) at the top of the demand curve and toward one in which smaller niche companies, products, and services rule the zeitgeist in the "long tail." Your opportunity is in there, hiding behind the big stuff. There are riches in niches.

What does this mean for you? According to Anderson, it's good news for ageless startups because our consumer culture is moving away from a focus on big-box markets to one that favors niches. What he refers to on his blog as "one-size-fits-all containers" of consumers and products are being replaced by goods and services with a narrow target.

I have seen this in my own journey. One of my past businesses focused on providing custom banners for special events. In the early stages, we focused on college reunions. Colleges were spread out all over the place. Their reunions were only once a year. And yet, by carefully aggregating them as customers, one alumni office at a time, we were able to develop a sufficient cohort that generated orders year-round, year after year. We had supported many of those customers for more than 20 years by the time I sold that business to move on. Lots and lots of commerce lives out in the niches of the long tail.

In another example, I launched a small business to solve a problem that only occurred in several factories per state. The problem focused on oily contamination of critical manufacturing fluids in heavy manufacturing processes. This caused significant production issues, as well as large amounts of air and water pollution. We hammered on that solution at the first customer's plant (thank you, Harley-Davidson!) until we perfected the solution. That customer told other factories with this problem about our solution, and slowly, we were able to add a sufficient number of customers around the country, not connected to one another except that they shared this particular problem. By the time I was done and moving on, we had similarly isolated niche customers all over the world from Beijing to Johannesburg, from South America to Europe and across North America. These systems ended up being used in tiny niche applications from spacecraft manufacturing to gear hardening for marine engines. This was not a unified market. We picked up customers with similar problems across the expanse of the long tail. Along the way, we were awarded the United States Small Business New Product of the Year and *Fast Company*'s award for the most innovative companies in the world—all from scattered opportunities spread thinly across the long tail.

The world of entrepreneurship, especially for ageless entrepreneurs, does not have to be a crash course in all things new or the shiny object trend of the day. More often than not, businesses are focused on maximizing their systems, scaling, and growing market share doing what they do best.

This is where you come in. You can make a contribution with the knowledge, wisdom, and networks your experience has blessed you with. In other words, use what you know about the industries in which you've already worked with to create a niche for your ageless startup.

I recommend setting your sights on helping other enterprises that are industry-adjacent to your knowledge base. There are many opportunities and directions for building sustainable business models for your startup and for the organizations you are helping. There are a zillion niches that specialize in solutions for enterprises. Here are some questions to ask as you are identifying this potential customer base:

▶ If you know insurance, how can you help other small businesses learn more through you?

▶ If you were an administrator, how can you serve enterprises with administration issues?

▶ How can you help with the specialty you know best and are passionate about?

   – New business development

   – Marketing and sales

   – Networking

- Travel
- HR
- Accounting
- Media relations

From small to large, all enterprises are continuously looking for help. Usually, the bigger they get, the more aggressively they're looking for smart solutions.

Set yourself up to serve a highly-focused market you really love. Get great at your specialty. Expand your networks. Hang out with the smartest people in the field. Search out young people making smart new contributions to your field of specialty.

You can make your organization multinational on day one from your kitchen table. You can build a life for yourself with more control over your day job and your destiny. People and organizations the world over are looking for newer, better, unusually smart solutions. Good business models have never been more available. Perhaps most importantly, trend watchers understand that smart, sustainable enterprise is not only respectable (even chic!), but the core of what's coming.

CHAPTER 1 DELIVERABLES

You can start your ageless startup journey by focusing on three tasks: giving yourself permission, planning, and putting what you know into practice. In this chapter, I introduced you to the concept of ageless entrepreneurship and showed you that:

▶ *You are not alone.* There are well over one hundred million of us in the U.S. in the second half of life.

▶ *Your age is not a setback.* As an ageless entrepreneur, you have knowledge, know-how, and networks to help you build your enterprise at your own pace.

▶ *Passion leads to mission.* You know how to solve problems—especially ones that are part of your existing enterprise network. Focus on what problem you want to solve and build your mission around it so you can launch a new enterprise to match your goals.

▶ *Entrepreneurship can free you.* Starting a new venture can help you control your time, increase your income, and be your own boss.

▶ *You have time on your side.* As a seasoned career veteran, you have the luxury of starting slowly and staying small.

▶ *Opportunities are right in front of you.* This is the renaissance age of entrepreneurship, and it's just beginning. Older, wiser, seasoned people like you can become entrepreneurs easier and faster than at any time in history. You can create an enterprise that serves your own goals and aspirations while giving back to and growing the communities of interest that you love and are passionate about.

Now that you know why you should start now, jump into the next chapter to a take a hard look at where you really are in your ageless startup journey.

GETTING REAL
WITH YOURSELF

Retirement is becoming nothing more than a quaint notion for most people. The idea that most of us can amass enough wealth during our lifetimes to simply take the final 25 to 50 years off is no longer the paradigm most of us live by.

And it is not just a money issue. For those of us in the second half of life, the notion that you'll WANT to walk out the work door and stop contributing is distasteful. We professionals are carrying a lifetime's worth of knowledge, know-how, and networks with us. We can put those skills and assets to work for the good of causes we care about, communities we love, and ideas we are passionate about.

We may not live entirely off of these new efforts, but we can greatly extend the savings and passive income we have put in place after years in the workforce. (As a generation, we are luckier than our younger peers in that regard.) You can make a modest amount of money from a new ageless startup and have a huge impact on your quality of life.

As you read in Chapter 1, this book and this concept are not about creating an instant business success that gets you out of every financial difficulty you may be facing. This book is about starting small, smart enterprises that can contribute to your financial well-being while also creating a new platform for you to grow personally and professionally as you grow older.

So, how do you know if starting a business is the right path for you? And how do you know when the time is right to lay the groundwork for the next chapter of your work life? If your answer is that you'll figure it out when you get there, then you'd better start figuring it out soon. Creating new income streams with a new enterprise is entirely possible, but it takes time and resources. It is always best to start small, start slow, and start smart—with some self-assessment.

When you ask yourself some simple questions about where you'll be working at 60 or 65, don't see work as a burden to live through. See it as a path to liberation in the later years of your life. You can make an important difference in the lives of people in your community. More importantly, you can help secure a more resilient and flexible lifestyle that you can carry forward into your later years as long as you are able. Ask yourself:

▶ Do you understand that staying active and engaged is better for your health and longevity?
▶ Can you afford to invest a small amount of money to launch a new enterprise?
▶ Can you invest the time needed to plan, launch, and grow a small enterprise?
▶ Can you work through adversity?

Start asking yourself questions like these now so you can get ready for a future that is bright with opportunity and resilience. Sure it can be scary, but it's much scarier to have no answer at all to the question, "Where will you be working when you're 60 or 65?"

In this chapter, I will walk you through some of the most common questions people ask when they are considering a new business adventure later in life. We'll use these big-picture questions to help you take stock of your own situation so you can make those first moves toward scaling your idea into a new reality that will pay dividends for the long term.

 Ageless Entrepreneur Spotlight

Dreena Dixon, founder of Chiku Awali African Dance, Arts & Culture and 2014
Purpose Prize Fellow (New York)

Q: *What did you do as your first career?*

A: I began as a probation officer and traveled the ranks through the New York State Department of Correctional Service system to become the Superintendent of Taconic Correctional Facility in Bedford Hills, NY.

Q: *What would you do differently now that you've had some time developing your current adventure?*

A: Raise more money so the organization could truly become a sustained entity. I do too much and wish I had delegated more. However, I am a volunteer, and most of what gets done through Chiku Awali is through volunteers.

Q: *What is the best piece of advice you would share with someone in the second half of life considering entrepreneurship?*

A: Be mindful of your time. If you have a lot of it, that's fine. If you don't, don't become an entrepreneur or a volunteer with a nonprofit organization.

WHY ME?

Why is an ageless startup right for you? When you consider your options, you will likely see that the question perhaps shouldn't be, "Why me?" but rather, "Why NOT me?" Consider what you already know about yourself:

▶ You have skills and knowledge that have taken most of a lifetime to accumulate.

▶ You have the time to build a new career slowly and thoughtfully that can reflect the values you want to leave for those who follow.

▶ You have networks of friends, colleagues, and connections and that are unique in history.

▶ You have the passion to make a difference and time enough on the planet to not care what others think about you.

The bad news is that many people build walls around themselves to keep the changing world at bay. While that may be comforting, it's also self-defeating. Everything will continue to change, likely at an increasingly quick pace. It's no longer the status quo (if it ever was). It's the fluxus quo, now and forever.

The good news is that learning new ideas, skills, and information usually doesn't cost anything. You can do it on your own timeline and test that new knowledge in venues of your own choosing. Most importantly, you can teach yourself to live with change, especially if you are helping create some of that change.

Why should you start a life of entrepreneurship at this point in the game? Your entrepreneurship self-assessment should be focused on how you want to conduct the rest your life. When you ask yourself, "Why me?" and wonder if this path is right for you, here are a few questions to guide that inquiry:

▶ What goals do you have for your new enterprise?

▶ What parts of your life would you like your startup to enhance?

▶ What parts of your life would you like to keep separate from your startup?

▶ How much money can you invest to launch your startup? Make sure this is money you can afford to live your life without.

- What in your personality is most professionally important to others?
- Are there other areas of your personality that you don't want to expose to your customers?
- What milestones in your work life can you highlight as important to your startup?
- Are you willing to share your workload with other professionals (accounting, tax, etc.) or do you need to do it all?
- Are you good at meeting new people?
- Are you good at listening?
- Are you good at empathizing with people describing their problems?
- Do you have the personality that can see problems as opportunities?
- Can you refine your passion or mission into a single compelling sentence or two?
- Can you describe who the customers for your future enterprise will be?
- What problems will you solve for your target consumer?
- Can you motivate yourself and work independently?
- Are you comfortable asking for help?
- Are you willing to work outside traditional work hours?
- Can you learn to meet new people and insert yourself into new situations?
- Are you comfortable using social media, even at an entry level?
- Can you admit you don't know something when appropriate?
- Can you learn from mistakes and failure and accept outcomes that aren't perfect?
- Can you say no to people and projects that don't fit your business model?
- Can you work in business with people you may disagree with personally?
- Can you be satisfied with not being recognized as the smartest person in the room?
- Can you work in ambiguous situations, in which no clear outcome is initially visible?

Take some time to journal your answers to these questions or create a working document that you can return to later and review your answers. You'll likely find that the question of, "Why me?" is a multifaceted one that touches on several areas of your entrepreneurial spirit, reality, and worldview.

Older entrepreneurs can create significant value for themselves and their communities by focusing on the life skills and traits that got them here: common sense, tenacity, and a strong ethic of helping. You can apply your extensive knowledge of what doesn't work to bypass entrepreneurial roadblocks. You have the time and resiliency to launch new businesses that may be slow to grow but rich in benefits. You do not need immediate returns as many investor-backed startups led by younger thrill seekers do. You possess the self-discipline needed to see tasks through to fruition. By this time in your life, you have likely figured out what you are truly passionate about and can build new enterprises to serve those goals.

In researching this book, one surprise roadblock to success for older entrepreneurs is their limited contact with other entrepreneurs. Many people have led business lives outside this system. Not knowing other older entrepreneurs is a barrier to entrepreneurship for older people. That is one of the main purposes of this book; to bring ageless entrepreneurs together for mutual support, knowledge-sharing, and inspiration. If you need additional mentorship or coaching in specific disciplines such as accounting or law or insurance, you can find those skills in your peers.

Do I Need Work to Be Happy?

I believe sustainable work is not about making you happy. It's about work that makes the world a better place, executed in a way that pays the bills. It's about being useful. You'll find satisfaction in the contributions you make. You'll find honor in developing work you are passionate about. That's the path that's sustainable.

If you rely on gaining happiness from your work, you'll be doing work that's meant to fulfill you and you only—not work that's designed to make the world a better place.

We need to create contributions to our communities and to the planet, not work to pad our self-esteem. Satisfaction comes from the life you lead, not the work you do. Focus on your work to make the life you want to lead possible.

Happiness in business is typically portrayed in the media as ruthless moguls gleefully crushing little competitors. Of course that landscape exists, but it does not define happiness, especially in the world of ageless startups. Satisfaction is an internal reward and one you earn by delivering your best work. It's also a feeling far superior to transitory happiness because it means you've made a contribution of your design. You've changed the world in however many small ways your dream will roll out.

You don't need anything more on your resume. You don't need awards or adulation. You need to make a difference. You can accomplish that through effort, disappointment, determination, and grit. That's why they call it work. If happiness is to come from your work, let it happen with those receiving the benefits of your efforts.

Your goal is not happiness. Your goal is satisfaction. Satisfaction that is internally driven and that creates further motivation to continually get better and more valuable at what you do.

WHY NOW?

Many people want to start their own enterprise, but they never begin because they just can't seem to find the perfect time. The most common reason I've seen over the years is that people just don't give themselves permission to try right now. While many young people openly consider entrepreneurship as a career option, many of their older peers don't have that same mindset. The media does a great job of promoting youthful entrepreneurship, but there is not a comparable narrative in our culture supporting older entrepreneurs.

As older people, we often wonder how we will fit in as entrepreneurs, how to present ourselves as startups, or how to position our new enterprise showing our age as an asset. These are false hurdles. We don't need to doubt our competency or our right to make a difference. We need to give ourselves permission to explore entrepreneurship on our own terms. The reality is our life experiences are all the permission we need. We don't need to question our abilities. You are capable just the way you are. You have the knowledge, networks, and know-how without asking anyone for permission. The rest are just details you can learn. It's not hard. It's just new.

Part of the reason for this is that too many people are put off by the language of business they haven't needed before because they've spent their lives working to make someone else rich—phrases like market research and business plans, financing and profit-and-loss statements, and on and on. It all sounds like too much to learn quickly, especially if you're ready to dig in right away. These planning steps are needed, of course, but only when your organization grows, so don't let your lack of hardcore planning up to this point stop you from getting started now.

Why? Because these are all things you can learn. There are free online courses in everything from the most basic bookkeeping, to case studies of small businesses around the world, to sales and marketing help. There are services that can help (and you can even start one of these services in your own field!) like your local Small Business Development Center (SBDC) or Small Business Administration (SBA) office. There is even the old-fashioned, get-a-book-from-the-library way. You don't need a degree from Harvard Business School to do this. You need yourself, your passion, and your dedication—not a perfect time to start.

In thinking about timing, ask yourself:

TIP

Most people who consider entering this fray can do a self-funded, slow startup with little or no money. You can also start your enterprise in a way that fits into your own schedule, with realistic expectations for growth.

- ▶ Do you feel that your current situation at work is guaranteed for the rest of your life?
- ▶ Do you feel that outside forces—business, politics, life—could disrupt the organization you work for in ways that are not in your self-interest? If so, is the time right to create an exit strategy?
- ▶ Do you have 10 or 20 hours per week to explore your new ideas for a startup?
- ▶ Will your immediate family support your entrepreneurship exploration?
- ▶ Most small businesses are self-financed with small amounts of money. Do you have access to a small nest egg (a thousand dollars or so) to launch initially and cover some basics like legal

registrations, some travel perhaps, business cards, etc.? This money needs to be fully separate from your personal budget requirements.

If you are in the second half of life and have some financial stability built in, your time is now. Go for it. If you are a younger ageless entrepreneur with a day job and an eye on the post-9-to-5 horizon, unless you're flush with plenty of cash to carry you through your startup, I don't recommend quitting your job and plunging in headfirst. You should take a breath and assess what's in front of you. Starting a side gig is an ideal way to launch your entrepreneurial life. If you're able to put a self-enterprise project in place that can fit into your life sustainably, shouldn't you at least think about it?

For most people new to business startups, the best answer is to start part-time. The internet has made this possible in ways that have never existed before now. You can work out the logistics, see what breaks, and build your way into sustainable cash flow.

What have you got to lose? In five years, you will be five years older whether you launch your enterprise or not. Why not be five years older (and wiser) with a five-year-old business, or at least five years of entrepreneurship experience? The time is always right to start thinking about your ageless startup.

WHAT ARE MY GOALS?

Life is not something you have to do. Life is something you *get* to do.

You are working on a blank sheet that can blossom into a new life of your own making. Quiz yourself. Write down your answers on that blank page. You may be surprised by what you find. Ask yourself:

▶ What impact to your professional life do you hope your new business will have?

▶ What impact to your personal life do you hope your new business to have?

▶ What freedom do most hope to gain from your self-enterprise?

▶ What impact to your target market do you hope your new business to have?

▶ How far do you hope your business's impact to reach? Locally, nationally, globally?

▶ What impact on your family do you hope your new business to have?

▶ What legacy do you hope to leave behind with your self-enterprise? For your family, your community, or your industry?

In considering your goals, it's important to think about your legacy so you can have a holistic picture of what your startup could look like over time. After all, your startup shouldn't leave this world when you do—it should ideally have a lasting impact. In a 2018 article, the science magazine, *AZO Quantum,* posed the question, "How much does the internet weigh?" The author posed that question to ponder the impact of the internet on business and society. (Spoiler alert: it's huge.) Similarly, as an entrepreneur, you can think proactively about how much your own contribution will "weigh" to the world. As micro entrepreneurs, you and I probably won't invent the next internet. However, it's interesting to ponder how much impact seemingly tiny contributions can make on the world. How much will YOUR contribution weigh? What legacy will your ageless startup leave behind?

> **TIP**
>
> The weight of your entrepreneurial contribution may seem small to others, but it can be world-changing for you and the people who will benefit from it.

Beginning something big shouldn't be measured by marble facades or employee counts. The impact you make is what's important. Ask yourself what you want to leave behind:

▶ Am I working to leave the world better than I found it?

▶ Is the work I'm doing designed to inspire and motivate others?

▶ Am I plowing fields for the next generation to plant their ideas and solutions?

▶ Does the work I'm doing matter to others or just me?

Ready for the weight of the internet? Here's *AZO Quantum's* measured conclusion:

"The internet comprises of videos, documents, and web pages. It contains a massive amount of information that grows every day. Every email sent, a comment left, and an article published creates more data which is stored in binary digits (1s and 0s) and read by computers . . . . Seitz

Ageless Entrepreneur Spotlight

Joan Beverley Izzo, founder/owner of Heirlooms Again (Illinois)

Q: *How did you find your current passion?*

A: My passion began at the age of 10 when my mother taught me to sew. I was thrilled to be able to make things for myself that no one else had worn first. As I grew up, I enjoyed making gifts for family and friends and really enjoyed being able to use vintage fabrics and linens in the process. As an adult, my husband encouraged me to pursue it. Due to family responsibilities, though, it remained a beloved hobby until I turned 50. My youngest child finished college that year, and a dear friend, same age as I was, died. With my husband's encouragement, and that of another very dear friend, I thought "What am I waiting for? Just do it!" I'm now 64 and just as excited as the day my website went live.

Q: *What would you do differently now that you've had some time developing your current adventure?*

A: I don't think there's one thing I'd do differently. I started small, started smart (getting advice from an accountant and bank, etc.), BUT I STARTED!

Q: *Are there any mistakes you can share from your own current career?*

A: The only mistake I can think of in my current career was selling myself short on my value to the owner of the business. Once I rectified that, I was able to make a big difference for both companies and their owners. And I found much more satisfaction in what I was doing.

Q: *What is the best piece of advice you would share with someone in the second half of life considering entrepreneurship?*

A: My advice to a person in the second half of their life considering entrepreneurship would be to find: A great advisor and accountant, as well as friends and family as sounding boards.

calculates that the entire weight of the internet is approximately 50 grams, the same as the weight of a large strawberry." What will *your* contribution weigh?

Press on. Measure yourself by your own goals and standards, and you can change the world.

Your practice is measured by its value to others. Forward.

HOW WILL I FIND THE TIME?

Starting your own business is not for the faint of heart. Running your own business is a full-time mental commitment, even if it is a part-time gig. You need to show up, do the work, still go to your day job, care for yourself and your family, and find time to eat and sleep every single day. Working only when everything else is done won't cut it. Everything else is never done.

If you are starting part-time as you phase your way out of the non-retired workforce, you can carve out enough time to accomplish something valuable every day. Look to your current schedule. Are there blocks of time you can identify where you do activities that don't further your biggest goals, like watching TV or endlessly scrolling on social media? Look at your productivity and time management habits to see when you work best. Is it early morning? Then set the alarm early. Do you work best on creative ventures at the end of the day? If so, form boundaries around blocks of time you can dedicate to them. If you don't block out these dedicated parts of your day, they will continue to be consumed by the middling little events of everyday life, and your journey will be stuck on a "someday" list.

For seniors, the transition can be easier than for younger workers in many ways. If we had children, they are typically at or near self-sufficiency by the time we move into ageless startup territory. Plus, our roles and responsibilities in our workplaces often are not on the front lines as they may have been at the height of our careers.

Perhaps of most significance is that many of us considering this kind of entrepreneurship in the second half of life don't need the income from our startup to pay the mortgage or monthly bills. Help with those things would be welcome, but our startups don't have to carry the full load.

Ageless entrepreneurs can devote their time to research, launch, and grow their businesses in ways that startups of younger people may not be able to enjoy. By keeping our expectations modest, ageless startups can avoid the trap of raising money and the resultant need to work on other people's timelines, not our own. As senior entrepreneurs, we can appreciate that controlling our own time and our own schedules in many cases is as valuable a payoff as piles of cash.

The good news is, once the bug has bitten you, your work is all you'll want to do anyway. Keep a journal handy in your bag or a file on your phone to jot your ideas down. (No, you will not just remember them.) When your assigned business work time arrives, you will already have the next idea ready to work on.

Block out the time on your calendar, whether it's 4:00 to 6:00 in the morning, your lunch hour at work, your bus ride home, or 10:00 to midnight when your partner is asleep. Block it out, show up, and do the work every single day. (Yes, you might be allowed Sundays off, but you won't want to take them because you came up with a great idea over breakfast.)

TIP

If you're serious about claiming meaningful work for yourself, you must be meaningful about the way you approach it.

As you read earlier, 50 percent of owner-operated businesses in the U.S. work less than 20 hours per week on their businesses. According to the same report, 70 percent work less than 40 hours per week. As such, the myth of the over-caffeinated, sleep-deprived entrepreneur comes from somewhere, but it is an increasingly small percent of the entrepreneurship ecosphere. We as ageless entrepreneurs can build work schedules that fit our lives and capabilities. However, we do need to work professionally and to be available to the world if we want to make the changes we wish for and the additional income we plan on. When determining how much time you can dedicate to your ageless startup, ask yourself:

▶ Can you work during non-standard work times—evenings, weekends?
▶ Can you be comfortable working outside the typical 40-hour workweek?

▶ Can you carve out time from family and other commitments to work specifically on your startup?

▶ Much of startup communications come electronically (email, texts). Can you make time randomly in your day to address these communications in a timely manner?

▶ Can you carve out time in your schedule to return phone calls?

If you are working full time and transitioning into entrepreneurship, don't bite off more than you can chew. Plan your launch to fit into the time available. And lastly, everything takes more time than expected. Build in buffers in your expectations. Assume that everything will take twice as long as you initially expect, then be surprised if it doesn't.

WHAT PROBLEMS CAN I SOLVE?

Businesses succeed by solving real problems. Most people have no idea where to start.

So, what do you do? How do you pick the products or services you'll turn into your problem-solving enterprises?

Here's an idea I roughly guarantee: Look at the work you've done in the past. Where were the choke points? What were problems people avoided because of the work you did?

No matter how you spent the first part of your life and career, you've learned to be good at something. It can be anything from gardening in small spaces to designing fire safety systems. We all have a specialty. This doesn't mean you have to be the world's authority on a subject; it just means you can talk competently about solving problems in that niche of the world.

The goal of your startup's marketing efforts will be to find a sufficient number of people who are interested in that niche and then to connect with that community in ways that are valuable to them. You don't want to market to everyone. You want to market to folks who respect the value of the knowledge you have on a focused topic.

For example, when I cofounded an engineering-based business at the age of 45, I leaned on know-how and tricks of the trade I'd learned from my dad years earlier. I certainly wasn't the brightest guy in the field. I had far less exposure than other firms in that market. What I did have was a working knowledge of what didn't work and a history of applying what I did know to a wide range of problems in that general field. Other people didn't want to work in this area because they thought it was too hard.

The technology we were creating and marketing had an improbably small market size. Initially, there may have been as few as five or ten potential customers per state in the U.S. Because I was able to point to my past work in that field—particularly my knowledge of what *didn't* work—I was able to crack open that market and begin shipping systems. We soon controlled the U.S. market and began selling overseas. This led to our developing a devoted customer base on six continents and receiving numerous business and innovation awards—all because I had a really good idea of what didn't work.

You have skills you likely don't recognize or appreciate. Don't underestimate these. Do an assessment of your skills and then look for the small "long tail" niches to develop your markets in. Think about these questions:

TIP

Where in your field of competence are businesses having trouble hiring someone right now? It's a big country, and a lot of other businesses have that same problem.

- ▶ What problems do you continue to run into in the course of your own life?
- ▶ What are your friends and family frustrated over?
- ▶ Where are your own passions focused?
- ▶ What do you know more about than most people? In your business life? In your private life?
- ▶ Do the problems you see fall into defined niches? They don't have to be big; they just have to be real.
- ▶ What service could you offer to develop new ways to fix real problems?

Those are the ideas you can build your own enterprise around. Check it out. Actively wonder. Start a wish list and think about how you can solve existing problems and add value. How can you become the world expert at one single thing? Use the worksheet in Figure 2–1 on page 48 to jot down some ideas.

Figure 2–1. **Pinpointing Problems Worksheet**

Now is the time to start identifying problems you can solve and how you can create a business model around them. Fill in the blanks below to start crafting your idea.

I have sufficient experience and know-how to call myself a leader in _____

_____

_____ .

People with this kind of problem can often be found _____

_____

_____ .

My target audience probably uses social media platforms like _____

_____

_____ .

Relevant professional organizations and trade associations may include _____

_____

_____ .

Media (such as magazines, podcasts, and blogs) devoted to this topic include _____

_____

_____ .

I can collaborate with the following people locally to solve this problem: _____

_____

_____ .

Thought leaders I can connect with include _____

_____

_____ .

Figure 2–1. **Pinpointing Problems Worksheet,** continued

Potential customers include _____

_____

_____.

Join those conversations gently. Be polite and respectful. Begin gathering names of thought leaders and prospective customers you can potentially collaborate with. Contribute to the conversations liberally and openly without expectation of immediate returns. You are joining a long game, one that you can operate within to make the changes in the world you are good at and passionate about.

You can make a nice, sustainable national enterprise out of that solution. Maybe not by next week, but it's doable in the next few months and years if you're smart and careful.

WHAT IF I MAKE MISTAKES?

We're taught these days to *visualize* success. Like great athletes, we're told to picture our successes and they will surely happen if we believe they will.

Is enterprise formation the same as setting out on an adventure? Done right, you bet.

You visualize outcomes and look carefully for routes to get there. Like mountain climbers in unknown situations, you sometimes need to change directions to stay alive.

It can be scary out there. Statistics come from someplace, and outcomes aren't certain no matter how hard you visualize them. Assume mistakes and danger are in your path and approach them with wisdom and care, not money and speed.

Instead, think about what will happen if you are not successful. How does that change your plan? What can you build into the process to turn mistakes into benefits? This focuses you on what works best and what actions REALLY get you closer to the outcome you've worked toward.

If you want to start a new enterprise and you have some doubts and fears about the adventure, good! You're human. Take those first steps slowly and wisely. If the outcome is worth it, there should be uncertainty in getting there. If the outcome were certain, it wouldn't be worth the effort. It would just be more of the same.

> **TIP**
>
> Start early and start carefully. Get yourself launched and start exploring paths to build the outcomes you want.

Do you have the stamina to live with the imperfect? The life of an entrepreneur is a life of imperfect plans, imperfect outcomes, imperfect customers, and imperfect cash flow. Setbacks and wrong turns are woven into entrepreneurship along with all the joys and gains that occur.

Failure itself is an integral part of life. All of us fail at something, sometimes many things. What is actually damaging is not failure, but the fear of failure. You need to approach failure as your own learning curve. If you can draw wisdom from it, the experience will be what separates you further from "wannabe" entrepreneurs—those who don't know what you've learned by failing at something.

Think about how you feel about failure and rate yourself in the worksheet below in Figure 2–2.

Figure 2–2. **Failure Assessment Worksheet**

Assess how you feel about failure. Then reflect on what that means to you as you embark on your ageless startup journey. Using a five-point scale, with 1 being "not at all" to 5 being "absolutely," see where you fall when it comes to your comfort level with failure. Ask yourself the following questions:

Can you live with failure?

> 1   2   3   4   5

Can you get over failure and keep your forward progress underway?

> 1   2   3   4   5

Figure 2–2. **Failure Assessment Worksheet,** continued

Can you see failure as a learning tool?

1   2   3   4   5

Can you see the value of the Thomas Edison quote, "I have not failed. I've just found 10,000 ways that won't work."

1   2   3   4   5

Can you recognize mistakes as experiments to be improved on?

1   2   3   4   5

Can you see mistakes as roadmaps to better solutions?

1   2   3   4   5

Now, considering your comfort level with failure, go deeper and think about how you might handle it when it happens (and it will). If the space allowed here isn't enough, you can grab your journal or open a new document and answer the following:

Write down a failure you've experienced and how you handled it. _____

_____

_____

Now, write down how you would handle it differently._____

_____

_____

What failure are you most afraid of when thinking about your ageless startup? _____

_____

_____

Why do you think that scares you? _____

_____

_____

Figure 2–2. **Failure Assessment Worksheet,** continued

What steps should you take to prevent the failure? Where should you go for help? _____

_____

_____

Mistakes and failures are inevitable when creating something new. If the right ways to the solution were already known, it wouldn't be new. You are inventing a new future, and that requires course corrections at almost every turn in your path. Can you see mistakes as opportunities to make better informed progress rather than setbacks to mourn?

 Ageless Entrepreneur Spotlight

Reverend Dr. Young Lee Hertig, cofounder and executive director of Innovative Space for Asian American Christianity (ISAAC) and 2015 Purpose Prize Fellow (California)

Q: *What would you do differently now that you've had some time developing your current adventure?*

A: I could have utilized a business coach 10 years ago rather than in the last three years. My academic work has not prepared me for Executive Directorship of managing ISAAC, a nonprofit organization.

Q: *What is the best piece of advice you would share with someone in the second half of life considering entrepreneurship?*

A: I'd encourage a potential entrepreneur to equip herself/himself with financial literacy and basic accounting as finance is crucial in delivering missions. Second, learning healthy views of asking and receiving donations from the beginning to help fly your dream. Third, enroll in financial literacy program and organizational leadership program.

One of my very best customers in a previous business was Harley-Davidson in Milwaukee. I was talking with a friend who worked there about all the mistakes I made trying to solve a problem for them with some equipment I'd helped design. In the end, the solutions were simple, but it took a lot of mistakes to get there—to get to simple. I told my friend, "Any idiot could have done it."

My friend's response was perfect. It sums up my approach to getting things done by well-informed trial and error. He said, "Sure, maybe any idiot could have done that. But you're that idiot!"

That's my kind of compliment!

Independent entrepreneurship REQUIRES mistakes to find new ground, to be smarter about innovation, and to be willing to do it until it's simple. You're worth it. Your outcomes are worth it. Give yourself permission. Take measured chances. Be that idiot!

WHICH CUSTOMERS SHOULD I FOCUS ON?

The biggest risk most new entrepreneurs build into their lives at the outset is choosing the kind of customer they will target. The obvious first guess—although wrong—is to target consumers as your core market.

I have tried this with many of my ventures, and it has always proven to be far too great a risk for the returns they generate. Business-to-consumer sales (B2C) are expensive, time consuming, and typically generate insufficient revenue for startup businesses. The buzz you often hear is about how big the consumer market is and how small a share you need to succeed. The reality is that consumer sales are profoundly expensive. You need deep pockets and a tolerance to risk significant resources to develop and grow a B2C consumer following. Selling direct to consumers builds in financial risks that, when taken, can sink your new organization almost as soon as it launches. Here are some questions you can ask yourself:

- ▶ What problem at your current or most recent work do you have a solution for?
- ▶ Can you sum up that problem into a single sentence or one critical pain point?
- ▶ Can you present your solution to that problem in a single sentence?

▶ Approximately how much value would you bring to a company with your solution?

▶ Would businesses who hire you need or want repeat business, or can they refer you?

▶ Do you know similar businesses with the same or a similar problem you've solved?

▶ Do you know of businesses across industry lines that might have the same or a similar problem you'd solve?

▶ If you were to create an elevator pitch for your solution, what would you say?

▶ Are there vendors or partners with whom you've built relationships that could refer your product or service to businesses that need your help?

If you become the next big thing with consumers, you can just as quickly become yesterday's news. Something faster, shinier, and newer will come along tomorrow. There are endless global competitors chasing the market for consumer dollars. While you may be able to carve out a niche in this world, others will see it soon and focus on taking it from you. If you find that you are passionate about creating a novel consumer product, I highly recommend that you find a business that is already operating in that space and sell it through them. Is this risky? Sure, but it's much riskier throwing your limited assets into a fight where you are outgunned from every direction.

For smaller, self-funded startups, selling services and goods business-to-business (B2B) is a far less risky bet. A startup, especially a self-funded ageless startup, needs margin. Margin is the difference between what it costs to deliver your product or service and what you charge for it. You need margin to be profitable. You can't make up losses by selling more volume. You may read about this approach with venture-funded tech companies, but it won't work for you (and it usually doesn't work for them, either).

Consumers are bombarded with options for more stuff constantly. As an ageless entrepreneur you are not selling stuff. You are selling highly specific knowledge, know-how, and networks. Don't sell stuff. Sell yourself. Sell your unique knowledge and abilities. Certainly there can be specific consumer markets for this information, but you will need to focus your sales and marketing on that specific subset. Most consumer markets are made up of wishes and dreams. Don't think you can stay ahead of the spin machines that manufacture these.

Businesses have problems that need solutions. Good solutions backed with good, honest service will stand out and engender loyalty. Businesses and organizations have problems they need to solve. They will pay you to solve them. Most ageless startups won't have to generate returns that satisfy investors; they will need to create income that serves your purposes and goals as the entrepreneur. Look for ways to prove your value to a small subset of businesses or organizations in your target market initially. Then, leverage those successes to the wider world where similar businesses operate. Word of mouth is as old as the first civilizations and more valuable than any marketing tool you can buy. Leverage your strength as a small-scale entrepreneur with great ideas. Nothing beats that story.

For small startups, especially those led by ageless entrepreneurs, a focus on selling B2B provides your best chance of having your solutions considered and sales closed. Your goal is not to generate a lot of press or social media about your new enterprise. Your goal is to close deals, provide the product or service, send invoices, and deposit payments. Every step of that process with B2C sales is harder than creating those same outcomes with businesses and organizations. There are far fewer organizations than there are consumers, but those businesses have money to solve problems and are willing to take a chance on entrepreneurial solutions. You need to get your early-adopter customers in place, and then just march down the list of related organizations with the story that you've helped their peers. You need to open doors—not manufacture consumer dreams.

DO I HAVE WHAT IT TAKES?

It often seems like the hardest thing you can do is to boldly begin something new. Yet the most rewarding, life-enhancing thing you can do as a human being is to begin something new and productive in your life, to do the work you were put on this earth to do, and make the contributions you need to make.

Boldness does have genius, magic, and power in it. The power comes from taking those first new steps. That's what makes the difference. Be bold. Plan, prepare, start.

But don't confuse boldness with risk. The old way of thinking about starting your own business was that it was a very risky undertaking. The newer, smarter way of thinking about startups is the exact inverse. It is much riskier to NOT start your own enterprise under the current economic circumstances. You don't need to keep all your eggs in one basket. You can diversify your options and diversify your income opportunities without spreading your risks. You are exposing yourself to unexpected job loss and loss of control over your financial future. Do you really want to leave your future to the whims of the market? A new analysis in 2018 by ProPublica and the Urban Institute shows more than half of older U.S. workers are pushed out of longtime jobs before they choose to retire, suffering financial damage that is often irreversible.

Entrepreneurship is a game plagued with a lot of myths and assumptions. Those myths can often lead new entrepreneurs and untested small-business owners right over a cliff. But you are an ageless entrepreneur. You've seen it all, and you can stand firm on the side of that cliff because it doesn't scare you one bit.

Another assumption about risk is that successful entrepreneurs are risk-takers (going along with the notion that starting a business is a risky venture). I have found the opposite is true. I worked tirelessly to remove risk in my businesses before my products or services hit the market. Most successful entrepreneurs want to avoid additional risk. The rest of our lives are full of risk. Why add to it?

The reality is that entrepreneurship is an exercise in avoiding unnecessary risk. Doing any kind of startup implies risk. Work to reduce your risk, not add to it. Make small bets that you can absorb if you've bet wrong. Take stock of the economic climate and industry in which you are starting your business, and then make bold, smart moves to mitigate your risk.

Think about it like this: The security that used to be the hallmark of large companies is

TIP

Give yourself permission to be bold. Create, build, and grow your plan. Your knowledge becomes the magic that infuses the enterprise.

long gone in the U.S. economy. This broken macroeconomic mess is a risk to all of us. However, broken stuff is also the surest place to look for opportunities. The security we all want is in our own hands. Everyone has marketable skills they can deploy in the service of fixing problems. This is where you harness the power of boldness.

Who knows where the current economic, political, and social crises will lead? I'm not going to tell you that small-business startups all lead to their business owners skipping off to a happy ending. I am going to tell you that if you don't boldly plan and start your own enterprise, your financial security will be at greater risk in the coming years. Period.

You may make less money. You may make more. You will have more control over your time. You will have more personal say over your own economic security.

Tell me what's risky about that.

So, are you bold? Think on this short self-reflection in the worksheet shown below in Figure 2–3 and consider what boldness looks like for you.

Figure 2–3. **Boldness Assessment Worksheet**

Answer the following questions below to get in touch with your bold side. Are you bold? Let's find out.

Bold entrepreneurs don't bet the farm. They work to minimize risk and maximize value. Doing things that increase risk is for amateurs. How can you minimize risk and maximize value for your ageless startup? _____

_____

_____

Boldness does not mean you are the loudest voice in the conversation. Those people are typically the ones with the least valuable contributions to make. Boldness means that you see a clear path to success and plan to travel it—not that you just talk about it. How can you show boldness without being the loudest voice in the room? _____

_____

_____

Figure 2–3. **Boldness Assessment Worksheet,** continued

Boldness means speaking with confidence. Boldness means you can describe the opportunity from a new perspective. The truth is the boldest thing you can share. How can you speak truth to your customers and other stakeholders? _____

_____

_____

Boldness is a secret power. Using it without the ability to deliver leads to failure. Applying this secret power gently, with value for all involved, creates magic and progress. How can you use your boldness in ways that create value for your stakeholders? _____

_____

_____

Bold startups work to reduce risk by gathering and sharing as much information as possible. There is no risk in being transparent. Just the opposite. Transparency and collaboration with others increases the confidence of all involved in any transaction. What are some ways you can be transparent with your customers and other stakeholders? _____

_____

_____

There is no hubris in being bold if you know what you're doing. Confidence, honesty, and transparency are 21st-century sales tools.

Boldness is a superpower. Use it.

AM I READY TO BOOTSTRAP?

Anyone who tells you it's easy to start and run your own enterprise is lying. If they say anything about fast money, run.

The reality is not like that. Startups can be hard if you don't set yourself up with strong self-awareness and resources. Birthing a new organization takes harder work and longer hours than you'd imagine. Sustainable cash flow is slow to build. The ability to capture and bank the profit can be even tougher.

For you and me, that's good. For the people who won't make the effort, that's bad. Starting and growing sustainable enterprises has never been easier, but the tools and the rules need careful attention.

This is why ageless startups should launch and develop as bootstrapping organizations. *Bootstrapping* means paying strict attention to sustainable cash flow and getting by with less capital at the outset. By building your enterprise around sales to your target market, you have your finger on the pulse of what's working and what's not. Early-stage financial planning should focus on day-to-day sales and profitability.

For ageless startups, skipping these hard stages to make easy money is a fool's dream. If you try to jump past the critical development stages— where you are learning your trade under live-fire conditions—you will miss the opportunity to hone your craft and become the professional you want to become. Fast money obtained through loans, investors, etc. can mask real issues you need to know about and resolve—plus, they greatly increase your financial risk.

Thomas Edison earned almost 1,100 patents. He said that to invent you needed a good imagination and a pile of junk. I am genetically coded to this school of thought.

However, what I think Edison really brought to the table was his determination and work ethic. He just kept showing up. He just kept making the campground better. Most of his patents were not original work. They were generally improvements in pre-existing stuff. Thomas Edison just kept making everything around himself better, easier to manufacture, and easier to use. In short, he learned how to bootstrap his operation.

Edison looked everywhere for opportunity, and he found it almost every place he looked.

When asked about this subject, Edison is widely believed to have said, "Opportunity is missed by most people because it is dressed in overalls and looks like work."

So it goes with your own sustainable work. It's dressed in overalls. It's work, trouble, and effort. So, ask yourself if you are ready to rely on little more than your business acumen and cash-on-hand by bootstrapping your new enterprise. Here are some questions to consider:

- Can you accept the hard work of learning through failure?
- Can you spend the time it takes to create great solutions?
- Are you using your new enterprise to solve problems or attract adulation?
- Can you build something from the ground up with little cash-on-hand?
- Are you secure enough in your personal finances to survive the startup phase without needing income from your ageless startup?
- Does your startup require significant investment to create its product or service offerings, or can you start on a shoestring?

Long-term financial planning starts with short-term financial viability. As your ship sets sail, you will learn which blue oceans to steer into and which financial shoals to avoid. With this knowledge in hand, you can take the next steps toward longer-term financial planning that can make this journey a joy to be on.

Run toward the opportunity, not away from it, and remember to wear your overalls.

Maximize Your Undervalued Assets

This is not bet-the-farm time. That stuff comes true sometimes, but mostly in the movies. You've got to find components to the solutions you propose that are largely undervalued. Because you are not at a point in life where you want to risk the financial assets you have built over time in your career; you want to try to create something from nothing—to use the non-financial assets you have to build your ageless startup. Here are some questions you can ask yourself as you evaluate what assets you have in your arsenal:

- Do you have ongoing access to specialized data that could be put to a novel use?
- Do you have collaborators in your network with whom you could partner to leverage and increase the value of your offerings?

Ageless Entrepreneur Spotlight

Dr. Murelle Harrison, executive director of Gardere Initiative and
2015 Purpose Prize Fellow (Louisiana)

Q: *What did you do as your first career?*

A: I served 40 years in academia at Southern University, the last 15 as chair of the department of psychology. As I began to think about what I would do with the remainder of my life, I realized that my teaching skills and what I had learned as a prevention professional could be used to make real changes in the Gardere community (Baton Rouge). Armed with more time and my knowledge of coalitions, I became the executive director of the Gardere Initiative, a role that positioned me to make daily decisions.

Q: *Are there any mistakes you can share from your own current career?*

A: Following much trial and error, I sought funds to establish an office in the Gardere community because I knew that making real change meant having a permanent presence in the neighborhood. Funds are needed for some basics, such as rent and utilities, but much can be accomplished through the development of relationships with people. In a one-year period, I was able to assemble groups of people, congregations, and organizations to offer a range of services that began to transform Gardere from a crime-ridden, impoverished community to a healthy community.

Q: *What is the best piece of advice you would share with someone in the second half of life considering entrepreneurship?*

A: My advice is to be guided by your passion. It must be something that gives you purpose for waking up in the morning and gives you a reason for putting forth all the energy that is needed during the day to fit all the pieces of the puzzle.

▶ Do you have unique vendors you can knit together into a specialized offering to your customers? Do you have unique skills or network connections that others in your field don't have?

▶ When building your new enterprise what extras can you do without?

▶ How can you spend less and do more?

▶ Are you comfortable enough with numbers to do the basic bookkeeping for your enterprise, leaving only the higher-level work to your professional network?

▶ Can you learn simple quote and order management techniques to decrease administrative costs? How can you utilize the new world of social media effectively without spending more on paid advertising?

> **TIP**
>
> What's your most undervalued asset? You! What's your second most undervalued asset? The networks of people you are already connected to.

Stocks and bonds and most everything else being chased financially are NOT undervalued. *You* are. Everybody has access to those other assets. Nobody else has access to your talents, your insights, or your imagination. Use these gifts wisely. Invest in yourself and beat the crowd.

CAN I BE CREATIVE?

Everyone wants to be creative in one way or another. For many of us seasoned professionals, work can be our outlet for showcasing that creativity. But is running your own business going to crush your creative dreams?

I would argue that creating a new enterprise is an outlet many of us find powerfully awakening. It's striving without a net. It is the ultimate creative endeavor.

Do you want to make a meaningful contribution? Do you want to build an enterprise that can create change? Doing what's been done before is not going to help you or the world. You need to build in creativity and sustainability.

Let's think for a minute about creativity, the role it plays in your life, and how you can apply it to your new ageless startup. Ask yourself:

TIP

You choose how to design your enterprise. You build it around cutting corners and screwing people, or you build it around service, creativity, and doing enterprise that makes a positive difference.

- ▶ Can I learn to be motivated by the discomfort of leaving the beaten path?
- ▶ Am I ready to create new relationships with people I haven't met yet?
- ▶ Am I willing to try—and fail—and try again to create better solutions to problems?
- ▶ Am I willing to suspend the safety net of 'what we've always done'?
- ▶ Can I look at problems and see opportunity?

You can't express your creativity and hope it pays. You need to express your creativity and *make* it pay. So, come up with good solutions to problems, good plans, good numbers, and good processes and procedures. This is how you get to creativity, personal growth and, best of all, a good night's sleep.

CHAPTER 2 DELIVERABLES

As I've met with aspiring entrepreneurs over the years, I've learned the hardest single thing they need to do is give themselves permission to explore the subject. We lock ourselves out of this option without knowing the reality of it. We bring the baggage of media myths about entrepreneurship to the table and assume we can't meet those metrics. These are false barriers that need to be broken down. As you explore the possibilities of your new life as an ageless entrepreneur, keep these self-assessment points in mind:

- ▶ *Follow problems to find your markets.* Sometimes, you have to look to where the chaos lies to find your niche.
- ▶ *Failure is part of the learning curve.* It's OK to fail—even when you're a seasoned professional. You can (and will) fail, so think hard about what your failure threshold is.

▶ *Define your goals.* You can't decide if a new startup is right for you unless you clearly identify what you hope to gain from the experience.

▶ *Reduce risk.* Maximize value. Are you ready to position yourself to reduce risk? You must decide what your risk tolerance is and what steps you are willing to take to reduce it.

▶ *Boldness is a secret power.* Be prepared to be bold. That's not to say that you must take chances that make you uncomfortable, but that you should harness the power of boldness as you plan your ageless startup.

▶ *Your goal is not happiness.* Your goal is satisfaction. As you self-assess, keep in mind that only you (not your business) can make you happy. But a well-run startup can bring satisfaction that carries over into all aspects of your life.

Now that you have a clear picture of where you are and what you want from your ageless startup, it's time to get started—slowly.

STARTING SLOW

I don't know many people who feel relaxed about their economic security. You may be in a good place now, but everyone knows that markets are getting ripped up overnight and there is little security in counting on what you may have counted on yesterday.

People want stability and meaning in their economic lives. There are certainly many paths to getting there.

A slow startup is a viable path for creating smart new enterprises that can make significant financial and cultural improvements in your life. Everyone wants viable new solutions, and the emerging model is competence and sustainability, not speed.

As you read in Chapter 1, a slow startup is one that organizes itself to work on the time you have available, not anyone else's expectations. You invest time instead of money.

Slow startup entrepreneurs don't first run to the bank or to investors. They value time over money. They get busy. Slowly. They introduce themselves to the community they want to serve. They learn the market ecosphere they want to operate in. They use time and knowledge to minimize risk. They plan carefully and realistically. They understand that stuff goes wrong and build that into their timelines. They build the internal support systems required to run a professional organization, no matter its size. They live below their means and accumulate real security over time.

Slow startups give the entrepreneur the freedom to get it right. Slow startups take into account your personal and financial status. This model allows you to build and test your own enterprise at your own pace. In the end, you will have a service or a product that you're passionate about and a sustainable business model that supports it.

Many people are postponing retirement not only for economic reasons, but also for reasons of personal fulfillment. Facing 20 years of the three Gs (golf, gardening, and grandkids—all wonderful things in and of themselves), many people choose to continue contributing to their communities through their work. Having more control over that work life can start now with a slow startup, started before retirement.

Slow startups certainly match up well with my own ageless demographic. Wherever you find yourself now, what's wrong with trying to create a long-term job by slowly starting your own business?

Ageless entrepreneurs are typically not in it for the adulation or big money. Most of us are following passions we have developed over decades and using our knowledge, know-how, and networks to change the world. We don't care if the people helped or the problems solved are not on the media's radar. We do it because we're solving a problem we care about. We do it because it's right, and it's a legacy of value we want to leave behind.

Most startups take far longer than people think. This is especially true for small, self-funded startups. That's not a bad thing; it's just what it is. What this should be saying to you is to start your own small business as soon as possible. It will take longer than you think to get underway. Start it while you have a day job. Start it in your spare time. I know this is not easy, but the time is there. Find what time you can, and put it to work.

By taking the process slowly, you will learn far more than by rushing through it. You will learn to enjoy the journey. And if you REALLY love this process after trying it out, you can circle back and do startups over and over by being a serial ageless entrepreneur—a perfectly viable and compelling career path in the twenty-first century.

So, start now. Start slow. Take some time to think about this and explore the possibilities. There are six simple, but critical steps to launching a slow startup. These make slow startups sustainable for the long term. In this chapter, we'll explore the initial steps you need to take to start slow to maximize your ageless startup's potential.

 Ageless Entrepreneur Spotlight

Bob Klein, founder of Festival of New American Musicals and
2014 Purpose Prize Fellow (California)

Q: *How did you find your current passion?*

A: I always had a passion for musical theater. Through most of my life, I wrote songs for my own amusement. In 1997, I became a founder of REPRISE!, a company presenting revivals of great musicals. We ran for 10 years. At that point, starting with WICKED, musicals came back into the mainstream. I changed my second career to the development of new musicals. The Festival of New American Musicals Foundation was born in 2007. I was 79 at the time.

Q: *Are there any mistake(s) you can share from your own current career?*

A: Not so far.

Q: *What is the best piece of advice you would share with someone in the second half of life considering entrepreneurship?*

A: If you had a successful first half, don't worry about the second half. Your experience will guide you. But . . . find a safe storage place for your memorabilia.

STEP 1: LAY THE GROUNDWORK

The first step on your slow startup journey is to get a realistic understanding of what it takes to wake up an idea, as well as the risks and rewards of entrepreneurship and how to plan for both. Ageless startups can be launched as smart, inexpensive enterprises, operated and grown at your own pace. Sustainability is the key goal.

First, consider the risks and rewards of your own new enterprise:

▶ Admit the risks you take by not starting your own enterprise.

▶ Acknowledge the risks you are creating.

▶ Set achievable goals for timelines and payback.

Next, map out the details of your ageless startup. You can do this in two phases: the first being a "blue sky" planning effort in which you focus on the big-picture details and dream big, and the second being an actual business plan (which you'll read about more in Chapter 5). Here are some steps you can take as you create your "blue sky" plan:

▶ *Create a rough outline of your business model.* What core product or service will you test first? How will you define that product or service so all parties will clearly understand the value and the proposition? Who are you targeting as your initial customers? What can you do to turn them into repeat customers? What problems are you solving for those customers? How much will you charge? How will you maintain ongoing contact with that customer?

▶ *Create a minimum viable product (MVP) you can release to test market your business plan.* This is simply a product that is sellable at its base level. (You'll read more about this in Chapter 5.) What problems are you solving? What solutions are you selling? Your initial drafts don't need to be perfect. They just need to provide you with a credible pathway into the market.

▶ *Build your virtual team made up of contracted professionals and advisors.* Surround yourself with professional advisors you can turn to (CPA, attorney, bank, insurance, advisors, etc.). This team consists of contract advisors who are not employees.

▶ *Begin marketing, networking, and learning.* Draw out your initial marketing and sales map. Who are your customers?

▷ *Determine the value of your product or service.* What selling prices are you considering? Learn to make informational cold calls to contact people who could influence your emerging business. Get their input. Learn and respect the educational and motivational value of "no."

▷ *Warm up online and start building your brand identity on major social platforms.* You don't necessarily have to have all of your startup ducks in a row to do this. In fact, building early buzz before you roll out the business is one way to get on the radars of your potential customers. You can start with something as simple as a very basic web page or Facebook business page. Post about your MVP there without giving away trade secrets. You can also let a small group of people know you are launching: friends, advisors, and thought leaders in the market you are entering. Ask them for feedback. Think of test marketing as commercial speed dating. Many people and ideas will pass by during this phase.

You should be comfortable with the amount and type of risk you are creating with your business launch. You should understand that you can start by offering products or services to your market that may not be in their final forms. You need to be comfortable with change and listening to criticism and suggestions. You need to be ready to adapt as you move forward. Your first idea is usually not your best one. Before you advance to the next phase—building your business plan—you need to be able to accept that startups are not hard, they are just new. As an older entrepreneur you have the time, knowledge, know-how, and networks to overcome these issues. Put them to work. Leverage the assets you've developed throughout your life. These are strategic advantages that are unique to you, the ageless entrepreneur.

STEP 2: SOLIDIFY YOUR BUSINESS PLAN

Next, it's time to begin transitioning your early-stage, "blue sky" concepts into a concrete business plan (which you'll read about in more detail in Chapter 5). Before beginning your writing process in earnest, learn what information you'll need, how to find it, how to store it, and how to use that information once you have it. You can do this by using appropriate business plan templates and industry-specific information to complete it:

- ▶ Search for free business plan templates online you can download.
- ▶ Search the U.S. Small Business Administration (SBA) for free templates and resources.
- ▶ Search online for industry groups, such as trade associations, that may have information and resources to help describe your market and populate the elements of your plan.
- ▶ Cold call leaders in your market to ask for information and further introductions that could help inform your business plan.

You will be more likely to succeed if you are prepared and recognize that your plan may need to change as you grow. Business plans are not sacred tablets from heaven. You can create personalized plans that fit your own budget, capabilities, and timelines.

Business plans come in many forms, but most contain the same basic outline. The U.S. Small Business Administration (SBA) has free outlines available online for both traditional and lean startup business plans at https://www.sba.gov.

The lean business plan is designed for relatively simple businesses like the ones discussed in this book. The SBA version utilizes a template called the Business Model Canvas (www.strategyzer.com/canvas/business-model-canvas). This model calls for you to provide information about:

1. *Key partnerships.* Who will you partner with and contract with to launch your enterprise.
2. *Key activities.* What are your competitive advantages in the market? How are you different?
3. *Key resources.* List the resources you will leverage to create value for your customers.
4. *Value proposition.* What is the unique value your company will bring to customers?
5. *Customer relationships.* Design your customer's experience with you from start to finish.
6. *Channels.* What is the mix of ways you will use to communicate with customers?

7. *Cost structure*. List the most significant costs you'll incur while launching your enterprise.

8. *Revenue*. Explain how your enterprise will make money. The SBA list includes examples such as direct sales, membership fees, or advertising sales. For non-profits, how will you attract funding or generate revenues?

Depending on how complicated your business is, you can tweak the format and style of your business plan over time. Remember: it's a living document, so adjust sails as you go. You can use your business plan to maximize your messaging about your ageless startup in these ways:

▶ After you launch, treat your business plan as a living document. Circle back and update it over time as you learn more through first-hand experience. Continuously update your plan with your lists of professional advisors and vendors.

▶ Check your reality against your initial forecasts. What's working? What's not? Why?

▶ Use the data in your plan to create your elevator pitch to describe your enterprise.

Once you solidify your plan, you can consider the 10-10-10 rule: Be able to describe your enterprise in 10 seconds. Then, be able to present your concept in 10 screens. Then, be able to provide a deep dive into your business to customers and stakeholders in 10 minutes.

As an ageless startup, the answers to questions posed in your business plan can highlight your experience, training, and all the industry knowledge you've gathered through the years. You can use your plan to highlight the breadth of the networks you've developed that can be leveraged to bring a unique value proposition to customers. Your know-how is an asset. Put these to work in your business plans. Your age is your advantage.

Your business plan is your road map. It is your guide to anticipating the questions you will face, the hurdles you may have to overcome, and the strategies you will use to grow your new enterprise. But you will not be doing this alone. Whether you've incorporated your own team from the outset, or you simply need the right advisors to help you launch, you need to know the ins and outs of building a truly supportive team.

Ageless Entrepreneur Spotlight

Colleen Callahan, founder of Colleen Callahan Consultancy (Illinois)

Q: *How did you find your current passion?*

A: I don't know my age when I found my current passion. It was likely inherited. My dad's philosophy was, "You come into this world with nothing, and you leave with nothing. It's what you do in between that matters." My mom lived the same belief. They were active leaders in our rural community and the agricultural industry. I chose to help people by informing and educating about agriculture through broadcasting. I learned through my experiences that effective communication is the key to understanding.

Q: *What would you do differently now that you've had some time developing your current adventure?*

A: I have no regrets. I still make mistakes, but I do my best to learn from them, as "Experience is what you get when you don't get what you want." Life isn't about your circumstances; it's about your choices.

Q: *What is the best piece of advice you would share with someone in the second half of life considering entrepreneurship?*

A: Never say never. Don't underestimate yourself. And don't be afraid to do something you've never done before.

STEP 3: SECURE YOUR SUPPORT TEAM

Support teams for small enterprises are critical. You need outside professionals to be a professional yourself. A great support team that fits your enterprise can be created inexpensively. Learn how to become a professional at what you do and where to turn for help. Here are some professional areas in which you might want to seek extra help:

▶ *Financial and tax advice.* CPA firms can help you get your books in order, set up your payroll, map out projected quarterly tax payments, and assist with yearly taxes.

▶ *Banking.* Ask fellow professionals and entrepreneurs what banks they use and their pros and cons. Focus on what you need out of a bank—lines of credit, ease of use for online services, merchant services—and let your needs fuel your decision when setting up your finances.

▶ *Legal.* Attorneys will provide expert advice and services, but for a price. For initial advice at startup, consider reaching out a local SBA for free consulting services to get started on the right foot and choose the legal structure that is best for your situation.

▶ *Insurance.* Similar to banks, your choice of insurance provider (or agent) should be based on your needs and preferences. Ask for recommendations within your network and consider what kind of service you need, your price range, and the scope of coverage your ageless startup might require.

▶ *Distribution.* If you are planning to sell a product, you're going to need logistics help unless you plan to store and ship items yourself. Look now for a distribution company that specializes in moving your type of product.

▶ *Marketing and Sales.* Unless you're already entrenched in the marketing world of your particular industry, you will want an extra hand with reaching out to your target audience. If you want to sell directly to the audience that best fits your product and/or service, you need someone who can focus on just that task.

▶ *Social Media.* Are you a social media maven? If you can't tell Facebook from Snapchat, you need help. Each social media platform has its own way of reaching customers, both in paid and free methods of outreach. Trust me here—find someone who knows the ins and outs so you can monetize your efforts on each platform.

▶ *Advertising.* It's not necessarily hard to place an ad in the paper or online, but an ad professional will know the best places to advertise your product or service based on your industry and audience.

Admit that you need knowledge, time, and resources you don't already have. And that's OK—professionals cut red tape you don't even know is there most of the time. Why wouldn't you? By admitting to yourself that you need help with these tasks, you can position yourself to make connections with these kinds of professionals by asking around for referrals.

Once you get in the mindset of networking, you can switch your focus to performing due diligence to connect with the resource people who will best serve your startup. Learn which outside professionals might benefit your goals most:

▶ Begin with CPA firms that will help you use financial best practices so you can position your enterprise for growth.

▶ Choose a preexisting banking relationship if you are currently satisfied. Focus on ease of use of their online banking services.

▶ Choose an attorney based on your personal circumstances. People with complicated financial and legal lives will want to make sure their new enterprise is adequately structured. People with simpler financial lives can put simpler plans in place. Many local entrepreneurship centers at tech schools, colleges, universities, and SBDCs can connect you to initial free advice regarding legal structures and ramifications to consider.

▶ Discuss your business plans with your current insurance agent. Ask for recommendations if they aren't a direct fit. Simple business policies to cover small-business launches are typically inexpensive.

▶ Explore the Small Business Administration (SBA) in your area. Visit local business incubators and co-working spaces. Learn about small-business support programs at local academic institutions.

As you narrow down your list of must-have resources, don't forget to use your existing contacts to make new ones. Ask friends in law, insurance, and banking for recommendations to consider. Be realistic about your value to professional firms. They need to grow their own customer base, but you will not be a must-have customer initially. Working with support team members is a two-way street: Help your professionals help you by always being as prepared as possible. Show them that you respect their time, and they will respect your goals and needs.

STEP 4: SET UP YOUR SYSTEMS

Next, you will want to create an internal management structure that builds your own confidence, deals with the details, and creates peace of mind for all involved. Start by creating sustainability with sound money practices, structures, and tools. For example, think about how you will keep track of your information like contacts, accounting, etc. Will you maintain databases on your own, or shop out the function to a CPA or financial firm? Either way, be sure to create a system to document all orders received, including dates received/paid, with full documentation of payment information. If you do it yourself, you can use a simple, homemade version (like an Excel spreadsheet) initially, but there are also many computer programs and online services like QuickBooks for order and payment management available.

Set up money and tax management systems that work for you. One way you can do this is to create a money map (like a mind map, but for your finances) of how money will come in and out of your new enterprise. Show your financial advisor (CPA firm) your money map. They can translate that into something called a *chart of accounts*, which codifies all the ways you earn and spend money. This is not written in stone. You can change it, but it should be as comprehensive as possible before you start.

Here are a few more tips for setting up systems that will help you keep track of your funds and ensure that you pay your fair share to Uncle Sam:

 ▶ Open a business-specific checking account. Apply for a business-specific credit card. NEVER mingle personal and business funds. Always keep a wall between them.

 ▶ Set up quarterly tax payment schedules. Check with your attorney and financial advisor for advice specific to your circumstances. Small-business owners estimate their profit for the year (including any withdrawals taken by the owner).

 ▶ Determine, with your advisors, if you need to collect sales taxes on the goods or services you provide.

 ▶ Request your Federal Employer Identification Number (FEIN) from the Internal Revenue Service (IRS). Even one-person businesses need this. There is no charge. You can apply online.

Remember: using your money management practices is not only important to the health and wealth of your business but also to create peace of mind. Keep secure records of all financial transactions so you always have them to refer to should the need arise.

Ageless startups will often be solo entrepreneurs (referred to as non-employer businesses) or small teams providing a service or products to a highly specific market that they know well. Just because we may be experts in this field does not mean we are exempt from the requirements of maintaining thorough and comprehensive business records. For that you

Ageless Entrepreneur Spotlight

Paul Tasner, CEO and cofounder of PulpWorks, Inc. and
2015 Purpose Prize Fellow (California)

Q: *How did you find your "encore" career?*

A: Fired by my last employer. Victim of the recession, age, and my not-very-well-hidden disdain for the CEO.

Q: *Are there any mistakes you can share from your own encore career?*

A: I thought it would be easy to raise seed funding. We had a great idea (sustainable packaging created from waste) whose time had come. Wow, was I wrong! Investors care only about their return: how fast, how big. The environment is quite far from their radar screens. Of course, I'm painting everyone with the same brush here, and we know that there are others. Hard to find, though.

Q: *What is the best piece of advice you would share with someone in the second half of life considering entrepreneurship?*

A: Get a business partner. It makes all the difference in the world. Celebrate together; cry together; advise each other.

will need to build detailed record-keeping practices that cover all aspects of your business correspondence, proposals, and financial transactions. With these in place, your life as an older entrepreneur will be easier and more efficient. You and your ageless startup will be assets to your customers. Without these, entrepreneurs of any age will quickly find themselves in a quagmire. Use your age to your advantage. You know that looking back is as important as looking ahead. Stop to document key data and keep your new enterprise sailing forward.

STEP 5: MARKET WITH MEANING

You've got the systems in place and your support team at the ready to help. Now what? Well, there *is* no ageless startup unless you market it. It's vital that you learn how to market and sell in your niche. Remember: marketing is not sales. Marketing is making everything you do in your business a clear window on the value you offer to your customer and then telling the world about it. Marketing is education. Teach people how your work makes their lives better. Here's how:

▸ Decide what you're selling in the broadest possible terms. Be able to describe what problem you solve in the fewest possible words. Simplicity and transparency in your offer is the goal. No surprises.

▸ Decide who to sell to and who NOT to sell to. A smaller group of targeted potential customers is better for a startup than a large universe of undefined prospects. "Everybody needs this," is a pathway to failure.

▸ Organize all phases of your marketing and sales plan around the benefits to be gained by your target customers.

▸ Identify the stages of client development and create marketing strategies for each: potential clients, prospects (those who have responded to your message), first-time customers, repeat customers, and market partners. Build transparency, education, and marketing into your entire enterprise.

▸ Build your marketing and sales program with a goal of enabling customers to recommend you to others needing your solutions.

You can also attempt to create your own "blue oceans" and teach people how to swim in them. A *blue ocean* is a market where there is clear sailing and little competition. To be a blue ocean in your industry, you need to:

- ▶ Understand, then ignore your competitors.
- ▶ Create new markets so you don't end up in the mud wrestling for your competitor's business.
- ▶ Use no-cost or low-cost marketing tools like social media and personal appearances to drive people to your website and then to your phone.
- ▶ Always ask for testimonials and referrals, then make those public.
- ▶ Be a teacher, not a salesperson. Use every teaching avenue available.
- ▶ Simple is the new black, so stick with the basics. You don't want or need bleeding-edge web presentations or hyped-up marketing. These are off-putting, and you can never keep up.
- ▶ State your solutions quickly and clearly, and provide easy paths of action for the customer to reach you (and purchase from you or hire you).
- ▶ Make everything people see, hear, and read about your enterprise simple and consistent.

Finally, remember that closing sales means making yourself easy to understand, find, and do business with. Most small startups will be selling directly to people in another organization, rather than to consumers. What tools should you use to reach them? Email? Social media? Phone calls? Define each channel you will use and then make a plan for each channel.

Because you are launching your startup in the second half of life, you have the time and patience to stop and do things right. You are not on a sprint to placate investors—you are on a journey to create delighted customers. Make your age into a business advantage. You don't need the latest whiz-bang business tools and techniques. You have time and wisdom on your side. Put those to work. Help your customers understand that your know-how, knowledge, and networks are meant to serve them and their goals, not yours. That's how you create loyal, repeat customers.

STEP 6: TRACK YOUR DATA

Sales and marketing don't mean much unless you can quantify them and analyze your results. Capturing data is a vital piece of your ageless startup's success puzzle so that you can turn those numbers into cold, hard commerce. Control your data or die.

You can protect your most valuable asset—your time—by organizing your enterprise data effectively:

- Start with what you know (word processing, spreadsheets, simple databases).
- Make control of your information a core sales and marketing function.
- Make yourself easy to do business with by having all relevant customer data available quickly.
- Accurately capture and store data to secure your past and create your future.
- Learn to write/type everything relevant and store it in an easily retrievable way.
- Keep all financial records in both digital and hard-copy form. Store backups off-site if possible.

Always accurately capture the most important informational pieces for business contacts you meet. You can get these from their business card. Transfer them into your own searchable system quickly. A searchable system is any tool or protocol you as an entrepreneur are comfortable using that stores information in ways that you can quickly retrieve it on demand in the future. I use databases for this purpose, but others may be more comfortable with spreadsheets or even paper-based systems. Databases are especially valuable in that they let you easily store not only full contact information and information about proposals and orders, but also complete conversations and relevant links to information about every person or business you deem important.

This is your business's intellectual property, so treat it wisely. For every contact, you should have easy access to the following information:

- Organization name
- Full contact name and title (as they prefer to be referred to)
- Street address (with office number if appropriate), city, state, ZIP/postal code
- Office phone
- Mobile phone
- Email address
- Company/organization website URL
- Internal company web page describing this person and their work
- LinkedIn address

You can keep a summary (be sure to include the dates of each contact) of all contacts with individuals creating outreach campaigns for each relevant sales prospect in your summary. Create, in advance, multiple tools in various forms of media—both print and digital—for contacting relevant prospects (such as email templates, postcards, sales letter templates, brochures, etc.). Finally, build an outreach campaign: greeting them with a light touch from your array of sales media.

Once you do all of that, you should turn your focus on creating and managing your quotes, orders, and vendor data.

Keeping Track of Client Data

Create and store searchable, comprehensive files of all quotes you generate for your product or service. It will both help and protect you down the road. Identify every formal quote with a distinct quote number, what is included, the date issued, and date "valid until" information.

Make an orders file where you can keep track of sales. Each order in your file should contain the following information (if applicable):

- quote number associated with the order if relevant;
- date received;
- all relevant aspects of the order;
- financial details of the order including relevant taxes, date completed, date invoiced, date paid, and payment information like a check or requisition number.

Keep Track of Vendor Data

You should also maintain files on all of your vendors. Each vendor file should contain the following information (if applicable):

▶ A distinct part or service number for every component that may go into your own product or service

Ageless Entrepreneur Spotlight

Bonnie Addario, founder and chair of Bonnie Addario Lung Cancer Foundation and 2017 Purpose Prize Fellow (California)

Q: *How did you find your current passion?*

A: While I was working as president of Olympian Oil Company in San Francisco, I was diagnosed with lung cancer in 2004 when I was 56. The survival is still only 17 percent. I made a promise to myself while in the lounger getting chemo that if I survived, I would do something to change this. Robert Kennedy said once about Caesar Chavez and the injustice afflicting farmers that, "If you are passionate about something, then do something about it." Here I am today, still on the job!

Q: *Are there any mistakes you can share from your own current career?*

A: I would have paid more attention to the caliber of people I hired. I should have believed in myself and hired people that could help me grow the foundation. I have them now.

Q: *What is the best piece of advice you would share with someone in the second half of life considering entrepreneurship?*

A: Life is not a rehearsal; we have plenty of time to sleep later. When you put your head on your pillow at night, ask yourself if you have made this world a better place to live. If the answer is NO, then go for it. You CAN make a difference. And, most important, never, never, never forget to LAUGH!

▶ All information about shipping costs and taxes paid for every component you buy from every vendor

▶ A list of price changes for components you buy from every vendor

▶ List of multiple vendors for similar products or services you buy

▶ Full contact information for all vendors and backup vendors

While it may seem overwhelming at first, setting up data capture and management isn't complicated—it just takes time. As an ageless entrepreneur, you can make time a business asset.

While storing customer contact information seems obvious, maintaining deep record-keeping practices that include retaining all past proposals and orders makes future interactions much more valuable to the customer as well as more efficient for you. Having every detail of past transactions readily available makes future sales more likely. Keeping information about all your vendors and how each one has supported specific projects makes future sales capture easy when the opportunity arises. As a businessperson, it also helps you keep a handle on changing products, services, and costs that you need to stay ahead of to maintain profitability. Your business data is your key intellectual property. Grow it, protect it, and continuously get better at utilizing it. Ageless entrepreneurs need to be knowledge hubs. Make your underlying business practices as smart and valuable as you are.

Take informed, measured steps. Develop mastery in small and valuable ways. Make as many inexpensive mistakes as you can as quickly as you can. Execute. Innovate. Repeat.

JOIN THE NEW ARTISAN ECONOMY

On the subject of starting slow, I want to introduce you to the concept of the artisan economy. This does not mean that we all become weavers and blacksmiths. In the 21st century, *artisan* is reemerging as a term describing work that is inspired by passion and driven by purpose. An *artisan economy* is also one that is inspired by the quality and skill of handcrafted traditions. It inspires individual entrepreneurs and small groups to apply new tools, new technologies, and new ways of thinking to help solve 21st-century problems with the same devotion to our work and craft that our artisan predecessors did. We artisans of the 21st century are not conquering mass sales markets; we are delivering our wisdom to smaller, more focused audiences who appreciate value over price.

I think of artisan entrepreneurship as developing your personal economic independence. With a trend this obvious, everyone should be thinking about their own enterprise using their own best personal skills.

You can follow this rapidly growing model to create your own new enterprise. Learn from published material. Follow entrepreneurs and innovators online. Begin the process by giving yourself permission to explore artisan entrepreneurship. Step into the process by learning to plan for sustainability and establish business practices that will serve that plan.

The access to tools and innovative business partnering is virtually limitless within the scale of small businesses right now. Business models— how you organize and go to market—are limited only by your imagination and adherence to applicable laws.

I type this standing under a photo of Buckminster Fuller who long ago predicted the ever-increasing utility of the knowledge economy, resulting in ever-increasing possibilities and pathways for all of us to make the world a better place.

This idea ties perfectly into the slow startup model I advocate: smart, creative enterprises launched in support of the greater good and designed to support entrepreneurs and their communities. This model addresses real needs and real problems facing your customers.

I started and ran a wonderful small business when I was still in college. My first business, Banner Graphics (which you first read about in Chapter 1), was built on my passion for helping recognize and celebrate people in their companies, organizations, and communities. I built the business around cutting-edge ink technologies and found ways to use them that no one else had thought of. I used emerging communication technologies at the time (the fax machine!) to create a marketing and sales system that enabled our one- and two-person business to serve devoted customers on six continents.

This business was never on the cover of any magazine. It was never used as an example of how to grow a large corporation. I developed a model that was the antithesis of growth at any cost. We grew the business to meet our needs as entrepreneurs, not a hyped-up version of what was deemed trendy at that time. I applied my passion for this market using new technologies to solve problems for 20 years. Our customers, many of them large multinational corporations themselves, loved to interact with our artisan enterprise—not because it was quaint, but rather because we solved a problem with all the professionalism and expertise they demanded in all other areas of their corporate lives. We were artisans. We were entrepreneurs. Above all else, we were professionals. This is the model for artisan entrepreneurship in the 21st century.

Our family developed this lovely enterprise until I approached the second half of life. It was time for the next stages of my work life and personal life.

Since the age of 45, I have launched multiple for-profit and nonprofit organizations, always keeping that "artisan entrepreneurship" model in mind. I've received numerous U.S. and foreign patents that resulted in the recycling of tens of millions of gallons of oil that used to be lost as wastewater. Our work has taken many tons of carbon-based pollution out of the atmosphere. And I did it all small and slow, as an artisan would, with a team of four people.

When I moved on from that work, I launched nonprofit and for-profit startups to create commercial solutions to local and regional food system development. This started as a one-person effort to transform a global problem into models that can be replicated at the local level worldwide. As of this writing, I am now working with small, energized teams that are developing some of the most innovative solutions to global food sustainability.

The Margaret Mead quote comes to mind as a recommendation for you to take this leap: "Never doubt that a small group of thoughtful, committed citizens can change the world; indeed, it's the only thing that ever has." This is a time of major transition in economies worldwide, and small-business entrepreneurs all over the world are emerging to lead the way to a better life for everyone.

Do what you love. Do what you feeds your soul. Do it passionately, and make it your very own artisan enterprise. "Artisan entrepreneur" is a great job title. What are you waiting for?

CHAPTER 3 DELIVERABLES

Ageless startups are an opportunity for you to grow personally while developing new revenue to support your life and your goals. You do not need to live up to any of the myths that cloud entrepreneurship. You can plan and develop a new enterprise that makes a positive contribution to the world while supporting your own goals. There is nothing bad about starting small and starting slow. In fact, starting and staying small is an admirable business model for ageless entrepreneurs. As you get off to your slow start, keep the following in mind:

- *Research is key.* Explore other slow startups and model your plans after their success.
- *Turn risk on its head.* Consider the risks of NOT starting your own enterprise. Doesn't it make more sense to go for it?
- *Warm up online.* Introduce yourself online early to build buzz around your ageless startup—the earlier the better.
- *Plan early with mission in mind.* Develop a business plan centered on your own mission and values. After all, the business is a reflection of you, so let your stakeholders see that, too.
- *You can't do it all.* Professional support teams are critical. Choose them wisely and thoughtfully.
- *Systems will help keep you on track.* Create business structures that work for you. Doing so will not only help your business run more smoothly, but help you keep your sanity.
- *There are riches in niches.* Learn to market and sell in your niche, focusing in on what you do best.
- *The devil is in the data details.* Turn your data into commerce. Good business practice means good data capture and control.
- *Create an artisan approach to enterprise.* In other words, craft your business the way an artisan creates new things.

Now that you have explored some initial launch steps, it's time to dig more deeply into what drives you: specifically, your mission, goals, and values.

SETTING YOUR MISSION, GOALS, AND VALUES

There is a widely used acronym that you may have heard of, KISS: Keep it simple, Stupid.

It's an old saying, and it needs updating. How about, "Keep it simple, Smarty"? Simple is the new smart.

A few years back at a startup, I was helping install a new piece of equipment designed to recycle industrial fluids. Our startup had landed its first few customers, and this factory was a key test.

There was a lot of science in what we had designed, but we worked hard to hide all that and make the use of the machine as simple as possible. The application was brutal, but the equipment performed above everyone's expectations.

What was most interesting was the response of the maintenance director. He had circled the recycler a couple of times while I walked him through the details. I needed him to like it.

He looked at me without expression and said, "This is really simple."

I couldn't tell what he was thinking. Did he think he overpaid? The recycler was ripping oil out of their production fluids. He had to see that. What was the problem?

Ageless Entrepreneur Spotlight

Edward Ginsburg, founder of Senior Partners for Justice (SPJ) and
2015 Purpose Prize Fellow (Massachusetts)

Q: *What did you do as your first career (or your most recent—or all of them)?*

A: First career: I was a trial lawyer for 19 years and a family court judge for 25 years before, reaching the mandatory retirement age of 70 in 2002. I am now 85.

Q: *How did you find your current passion?*

A: Current passion: As I approached retirement, I noticed that more and more litigants were coming to court without lawyers, facing the great disadvantage of trying to navigate the system on their own. As a retired judge, I felt that I was in a good position to recruit volunteer lawyers to represent the indigent. As my experience increased, I realized that lawyers were more willing to take on discrete tasks such a participating in clinics and taking on limited (as opposed to full) representation, Senior Partners for Justice now number over a thousand lawyers. Each week, I make a personal phone call to those who volunteered the previous week. The key is developing personal relationships and offering opportunities such as monthly luncheons with a speaker and opportunities to take courses.

Q: *What is your best piece of advice you would share with someone in the second half of life considering entrepreneurship?*

A: My advice is to enjoy what you are doing and be prepared to take on new challenges.

He said it again with no expression, "This is really simple."

Then he smiled widely, reached out, and shook my hand. "Thank you," he said. "Simple is exactly what I need."

Exhale.

Simple, in fact, is exactly what most people need.

You can apply the KISS method to the very foundations of your new enterprise. In this chapter, we will cover key ways you can set up your ageless startup's mission, values, and goals in a way that provides simplicity and clarity for both you and your customers.

DETERMINE YOUR MISSION

At the heart of every new enterprise is the organization's mission. A mission statement is a short, succinct statement about how you will position your organization to interact with the world. What is your business purpose, its meaning, and the basis of how you want your new enterprise to serve the field in which it operates?

A mission statement is not just an outwardly focused marketing statement, though it is that to some degree. A mission statement is also a very important internal tool for running your business. When you come to a fork in the road, such as deciding whether to take on a new customer or provide a service to another company (for the money or for its relevance to your mission statement), you have the guidance in hand to make that decision. You've put up the guard rails to help your future self live up to the potential of the opportunity. You know what your mission is, so you can create partnerships that reflect your values.

A mission statement should motivate you, inspire you, and be your key tool for presenting your opportunity to the world. Large businesses often write mission statements to please a wide range of stakeholders and end up pleasing no one. Because you are an artisan entrepreneur focused on niche markets, you can hone your words to speak to specific problems that inspire action in your own heart and mind and in the responses from customers you want to serve.

A mission statement should specifically cite the purpose of the organization, however inelegant and confusing it might be to others not in your target market. For instance, most people would not care about or even understand the mission statement I use for my current startup. It leaves out almost everyone. But the people who matter to this project will know exactly what the goal of my current work is and appreciate its importance.

My current mission statement is, "I want to make this region the artisan food manufacturing capital of North America." Likely, 99 people out of 100 will drift off as soon as they hear that. As an artisan entrepreneur helping lead a small startup, that's great. I've just saved myself a lot of time, money, and energy trying to convince 99 percent of the people who hear me when, in fact, they are not my customers. And that's okay—the one person who understands the message will search out our startup and engage knowledgeably and enthusiastically.

Lastly, it's important to remember that mission statements are not written in stone. Adapt them carefully as your circumstances, and your markets change. You may need more focus. You may need less. What you will need is a short, inspiring message to the world about the value you bring. Use the Mission Statement Worksheet on page 91 to help you map out your mission.

Write down what you would want for yourself with the KISS structure in mind. Your answers will help you clearly guide your new enterprise as it emerges. Your answers are not for others to read, but to see in your actions. Use as few words as possible to describe your core mission. You can revise it as you learn more. Ideally, it should be as short as possible. I use my own 10-10-10 rule described earlier in Chapter 3. The first of these 10s is your mission statement, described in ten seconds.

Your mission statement will be your guiding star as you sail into the future. Choose it carefully and rely on it.

IDENTIFY YOUR VALUES

What values do you personally hold dear? The new best practice in business is to emphasize our personal goals, values, and ambitions for changing the world in our business plans. In other words, focus on the emotional intelligence aspect of what we hold dear. By doing so, you will attract the customers you need and send those with discordant value systems off to where they belong.

Figure 4–1. **Mission Statement Worksheet**

The key mission of my ageless startup is: _____

_____

The service/product/benefit I hope to provide is: _____

_____

My target audience/customer is: _____

_____

My ageless startup is focused on growing this kind of business sector: _____

_____

I am focused on enhancing my community and/or industry by providing: _____

_____

My ageless startup can solve the following pressing social issues: _____

_____

Here is what I hope to accomplish for others with my new business: _____

_____

Here is what I hope to accomplish for myself with my new business: _____

_____

My mission (in as many words as you like): _____

_____

My mission (in as few words as possible): _____

_____

These are the values you need to use to steer your enterprise. Keep these simple. Be direct. Don't use extra words. The values you build into your new enterprise are values you must live by yourself. A sample values statement might be, "We will treat every customer as though they are our family, with respect and understanding."

As ageless entrepreneurs, we have the luxury of not paying attention to the newest business fads and buzzwords. Keeping your value statement simple and direct also allows you to be true to yourself and true to your business mission. You are working to share the values you are passionate about. Be clear, and keep it simple. The purpose of a values statement is not to impress. The purpose of your values statement is to educate people about what is important to you and your business.

Think about what makes you angry with business practices you encounter. What frustrates you about the way people are dealing with subjects you care deeply about? How would you approach the issue differently? Business practices are driven by the value systems behind them. Let this guide you.

As I approached my current startup, I was frustrated by the imbalance of support for nonprofits over for-profit enterprises in a vital area of food commerce. I was able to help steer our team to build our value system around supporting sustainable, for-profit solutions in this market. It's not that all the other solutions were bad; it's just that I was able to articulate a subset of the market we could have the most valuable impact on by helping identify the values we wanted to emphasize.

SET YOUR GOALS

With your mission and values in place, you can establish goals for the journey. How will you combine your passion, mission statement, and values statement to get the results you want?

You establish metrics you can measure. What steps can you put in place to meet your mission and the values behind it?

Following KISS principles, you will want to identify realistic goals that have meaning and consequence. As solo entrepreneurs, we need to include goals that benefit ourselves and our businesses.

Ageless Entrepreneur Spotlight

Tony Barash, chairman of the board of ConTextos and
2015 Purpose Prize Fellow (Illinois)

Q: *How did you find your current passion?*

A: I was 60 when I went to Uzbekistan and began to think seriously about the implications of literacy vis a vis civic institutions, democracy, and conflict mitigation. I was 66 when I went to Harvard where I became involved with the creation of ConTextos, a literacy, teacher training and conflict mitigation Non Governmental Organization (NGO), which started in El Salvador and has since expanded from Central America to Chicago.

Q: *Are there any mistakes you can share from your own current career?*

A: As you build a team (board, staff, consultants, vendors), hire slowly, fire quickly. In small teams/organizations, a disruptive personality can have a disproportionately adverse impact on time, morale, and performance.

Q: *What is the best piece of advice you would share with someone in the second half of life considering entrepreneurship?*

A: Forget about the trappings of the office to which you've become accustomed and learn/re-learn to do for yourself: the basics, the kinds of day-to-day things that, over time, others in your first career(s) were doing for you. Accept the reality of a multi-generational, multi-cultural workplace, and learn to communicate with the tools and in the vernacular of others rather than insisting that they communicate with you in your way and in your comfort zone. And, always remember that no question is stupid, whether it's yours or someone else's.

When asked if my work makes a difference, I answer, "Ask me in 20 years." The work is generational, not transactional. That's why I invest my time and resources in working with and mentoring young people. They will continue the work long after I cannot.

Your business goals should be simple, clear, and transparent. Your KISS approach calls for answers that are easy to understand for all who see them. A KISS version of business goals might look like these:

- We will grow and maintain a sustainable, profitable organization.
- We will add one new client per month for the next 12 months.
- We will answer all new inquiries within 24 hours.

Goals help you complete your mission. Goals help put your values into action. Goals make your new enterprise work. What problems lay in the way of completing your mission and the values that drive it? How would you get around those obstacles? How could you create a better system that would avoid or solve those problems? Those are your goals.

In my current startup, we saw wonderful small food companies operating at a disadvantage because they worked in seemingly competitive silos with little interaction among them. Even worse, there were few opportunities for collaborative marketing and to lessen supply chain problems for all involved. We set a goal to launch and grow a regional food and beverage network that supported the mission and values of the new organization, a network that could collaboratively solve problems for individual members, and one that could be grown in value and measured for the benefit of all involved.

When you look to create or grow your product or service, always look to make the interface simpler. You need to do the complicated execution and back office stuff better than anyone else, but the interface must be simple, or your enterprise will tank.

How do you know which goals will be most effective to help you carry out your mission? Reverse the design of your products and services. Reverse the design of your enterprise. For the specific problem at hand, start with your answer.

Build your goals with this result in mind. How have you made the solution simpler? How have you made the process easier? If you want sustainable work, think simple.

Mission statements, values statements, and goals should be written in service of honoring your passion.

Get that right, and you've got a high-value ageless startup.

SET A SUSTAINABLE FOUNDATION

John Byrne was the editor-in-chief at *Fast Company* magazine from 2002 through 2005. He then transitioned to Executive Editor at *Business Week* where he still holds the record for the most cover stories (58) in the magazine. He is also the author of 88 books including two *New York Times'* bestsellers.

I've held onto a phrase John used in an article for *Fast Company* called, "The Case for Change."

The phrase is "sustainable competitiveness." That's a potentially scary thought. You've actually acknowledged that you're entering a fray for which there is probably no clear victory. And there is plenty of defeat available. Byrne defines the kind of victory available to most startups and similar enterprises as simply, and sustainably, being able to continue on with the fray.

Gosh, *there's* an easy sell.

Actually, that's JUST what you should want.

You're probably not going to start an enterprise that will dominate its niche so thoroughly that you will be lighting cigars with folding money. Rather, you're going to start an enterprise that will need to slip into the weirdly chaotic commercial flood, stay there, and prosper. If you're wise, you'll even learn to love it.

My contribution would be that sustainable startups need to learn to live with symptoms like being messy, scary, exhilarating, and frustrating, as well as slap-you-in-the-face rewarding and impossible to predict. In this environment, you will need the ability to continuously go forward amid continuous challenge. In other words, you need to maintain a sense of sustainable competitiveness. There is rarely a true end game to this journey. My recommendation is to learn to create and then love your own great journey.

Many people won't want this kind of life. That's fine. It's not exactly an easy sell once you tell the truth about sustainable work. However, those folks are not who I'm talking to. I'm talking to the people emotionally nimble enough to dance on water and realistic enough to know that they have the skills and will to change the world.

The rest is *almost* easy, if you plan well. That's why it is vital that, no matter the size of your new ageless startup, you set a firm foundation with a clear mission, true-to-you values, and an achievable set of goals.

Competition and market chaos are healthy facts of life. Competition is the landscape in which you let your own mission, values, and goals shine brightest. You are not working against your competitors. You are working for your customers. As an ageless entrepreneur, you are bringing a significant advantage to the market with wisdom, know-how, and networks as your value proposition. Focus on your customers—the ones who appreciate and value the knowledge, services, and products you offer. Competitors with different missions and values will find customers appropriate to their models, which is fine. You don't want to be the enterprise with the most customers. You don't want to waste time with customers who don't value your model and your mission. Let them go. You want to be the enterprise with repeat customers who will consider price far down the list of things that are important when engaging you and your operation.

Your mission, values, and goals are at the heart of your business plan. You are setting a brave course to change the world with your unique knowledge and skills. Of course there will be chaos. Of course there will be competitors. That means you are in an active market. Use the noise to present your solutions quietly, purposefully, and with mastery. Your ageless status and the mission you create to share that knowledge are what will set you apart.

Create Mission-Driven Paths of Innovation

Sustainably competitive ageless startups can't be launched with the idea that you're going to repeatedly fool people into buying something. You need to fix highly definable problems for the benefit of the community you operate in commercially. You and your organization need to do this transparently and, to the best of your ability, elegantly.

In other words, define the problem and then innovate solutions that honor your mission and values. You need to set up your products and services so they continuously improve your community with ever smarter, ever more sustainable solutions.

Or as Douglas Rushkoff, author of *Get Back in the Box* (Harper Business, 2007), says, "A real brand relationship is like a subscription to a path of innovation." I like that a lot. Subscribe to a path of innovation. Sustainable solutions for the long haul. That's good planning.

Innovative solutions are what set your business apart. Innovation does not have to involve futuristic, gee-whizz inventions. Ageless startups offer those of us with years of experience the ability to cut through roadblocks that other organizations may be facing for the first time. That's the kind of day-to-day innovation that makes the world better. Innovation can be a new perspective or a new approach that others have not lived through or seen before. Ageless startups can be vectors of innovative thinking based on past experience and wide knowledge networks.

> **TIP**
>
> If you are to be sustainable, you'll need to honor the community you operate within. Be übertransparent and accurate with yourself and others. Define the metrics that describe success. Measure the progress you and your organization make toward solving the problems you've defined.

If you are launching your new enterprise to serve an industry you once worked in, you know how and where progress can be blocked. You know what stops people in organizations with problems from raising their hands. This is where your value can shine through the clutter. As a trusted outsider with deep knowledge of an industry or a market, you can offer pathways through the problems organizations face. You do this by presenting your mission and your enterprise as a solution that others don't have the experience, time, or capacity to resolve.

PUT YOUR MISSION, VALUES, AND GOALS INTO ACTION

My own lifelong entrepreneurial mission, values, and goals have revolved around solving problems that are significant but unpopular. And I have found that the secret to innovation is not the process of executing your ideas, but what precedes it. The secret to innovation is looking for

Ageless Entrepreneur Spotlight

Doug Noll, cofounder of Prison of Peace and 2014 Purpose Prize Fellow (California)

Q: *How did you find your current passion?*

A: The project began in August 2009 with a letter from a female inmate serving a life sentence without possibility of parole asking for mediation training. My colleague Laurel Kaufer read the letter from her mailbox. We decided immediately that we should try to do this. I was 58 years old at the time. I am 68 years old today.

Q: *What would you do differently now that you've had some time developing your current adventure?*

A: I would not change anything. The work is challenging the hours are long, and the pay is crappy. However, the transformations we have witnessed in thousands of inmates has been profound and immensely satisfying.

Q: *Are there any mistakes you can share from your own current career?*

A: Mistakes are a way of life. The secret is to laugh and move on. We work in an environment that is bureaucratic to the extreme, where there is no consistency, where security is para-mount, and where there is a huge range of cognitive and emotional competency. We make mistakes. The prison authorities make mistakes, the inmates make mistakes. We learn from them and grow. Be humble and gracious no matter the problem.

Q: *What is the best piece of advice you would share with someone in the second half of life con-sidering entrepreneurship?*

A: Follow your heart. Be courageous. Forget about the money. Bring light into dark places. Be persistent, disciplined, and patient. Celebrate the success.

problems other people don't want to solve or can't deal with. It seems like it should be more complicated, but I don't think it is.

I came across an old newspaper article about our first business, Banner Graphics, from sometime in the 1980s. I also had a more recent article about a subsequent business we'd started in an entirely different field. The captions under the newspaper photos were almost identical, though they had been published 25 years apart and were about two completely different enterprises.

25 years ago (Business 1):
"We're doing work nobody else wants."

25 years later (Business 2):
"Takes on the task almost no one else wants."

Innovate where the problems are. Problems are the raw materials of innovation.

Find the problems. Often, they're very subtle. Find one you think you can fix. Take your time. Do your homework. Work to understand that problem better than anyone else. If you do that, the solutions will become obvious, and then you can execute appropriately. That's my little insider secret to innovation. Mission, values, and goals revolve around problem-solving with your value system in place and measurable metrics to judge the progress.

CHAPTER 4 DELIVERABLES

Starting an ageless enterprise is not hard. It's just new. The promise of this opportunity for you is that you get to design your new enterprise around your own mission, values, and goals. You get to build a business model that helps you leave the world a better place. You can do it by keeping these points in mind:

▶ *KISS—Keep it simple, smarty.* Simplicity is the key to your success. Don't overthink your business idea or approach. Do what you do well, and stick to your plan.

▶ *Let your mission guide you.* Your mission statement is your foundation and your guide—don't lose sight of it.

▶ *Identify and celebrate your business values.* What you hold dear will be evident to your customers and other stakeholders as long as you drive your decisions with your values.

▶ *Create clear goals.* Have something to work toward, whether that is growth and scale or creating a lasting legacy business for your family.

▶ *Learn to live with ongoing change.* Be agile enough to switch your focus, move product differently, and look at your business with fresh eyes.

▶ *Search for problems nobody else wants.* This is where you can make a difference—and a profit.

Next, we'll dive into the details of creating your business plan and setting your business apart as an ageless startup.

CREATING YOUR BUSINESS PLAN

Professional Engineers (PEs) are not a notoriously funny bunch. They might drink a beer with you, but you wouldn't search them out if you were looking for the funniest or most madcap group to hang out with on a Saturday night. That's probably good, though. They are smart folk who are damn hard to fool.

The Society of Professional Engineers presented one of our companies a very special award a few years ago.

We made very rugged, simple tools for a nasty problem that plagued a heavy industry. Our field was oil recycling—separating industrial fluids from oily contaminants. There was nothing high-tech, not even a single electrical connection. You couldn't plug them in if you wanted to.

The night of the awards, I was convinced all the gee-whiz tech products would prevail.

They announced the winners from the bottom up. By the time they got to second place, I thought we were toast. Second place went to a very cool company that had figured out a new way to limit radiation needed for medical treatments. Even *I* didn't think we should beat this company.

Then, a most remarkable thing happened. The presenter started telling a story about his brother. He said his brother was a big deal. He'd owned several well-known businesses. The presenter said he wanted his brother's opinion of the winners they'd picked and showed him the list without telling him who'd won. The brother said every single one could win and remarked about how cool it was to have so much innovation around. But, his brother said, "Could you get me the telephone number of the guy with the oil recyclers? I've had that problem in every plant I've ever run."

The presenter quit his story there and said, "That's what we're here for. To fix problems, to make people's lives better." Then he announced our company as first place, best of state.

Simple stuff. Fixing problems. Get it?

I was supposed to say a few words when they presented the award. I should have pretended I knew something profound about innovation and technology, but I only had one thing on my mind.

"Thanks very much," I said. "Could I get your brother's phone number?"

We had chosen a problem that enough people understood. We had chosen a problem than enough people would pay for fixing. Critically, we had chosen a problem that when potential customers heard about our solution, they rushed to contact us.

Choosing the right problems to solve makes almost everything in your business life easier and less complicated.

I got the phone number of that brother, and we soon had another sale.

That experience showed me that when it comes to planning a business strategy, your own experience will light the way. Look for fields where your experience matters more than the chore itself. In fast-growing fields, there are critical, unmet needs that small service startups could provide.

Don't look to what's been done. Look for what's missing. Watch to see what's broken in the market. You don't have to be a specialist in that particular area. You don't have to solve massive, industry-wide problems. You just need to step up to the opportunity with the entrepreneurship, tools, and attitude that can address problems effectively. And, when you decide to map out a plan for that niche business that is uniquely yours, you will be well-positioned to showcase what is special about your enterprise.

For our team, the problem wasn't fancy or sexy, but it was one that needed our unique skillset, and we founded an entire business on it (and yes—won a few awards along the way). In this chapter, we're going to put rubber to road and talk about what you need to know to write a business plan for your ageless startup that showcases your own unique solution to whatever problem you've set out to fix with your business. While I am not going to cover every nuts-and-bolts detail of how to write a business plan, I am going to walk you through some considerations that are unique to ageless entrepreneurs.

BUILD YOUR ROADMAP

An ageless startup should be straightforward in its plans. We are focusing on ageless, solo entrepreneurs and very small enterprises here, and because of the typically small scale for your projections, there is no need to run complicated spreadsheet scenarios for investors. You won't have a lot of resources to burn up doing market research. Your goals for planning should be to keep everything simple and direct. You're not typically answering questions for outside investors. Solo entrepreneurs are most likely self-funded initially, so you are asking questions of yourself. You should be your most critical audience. Small does not mean it's unimportant. In this case, small means you need to be precisely focused on specific problems, methods, and solutions.

As entrepreneurs in the second half of life, we have knowledge, experience, and networks ready for those who need them. You can customize these questions to fit your circumstances, but you should be able to answer the essence of these for yourself and for future customers who will want to know these answers before doing business with you.

Simple questions. Simple answers. That's our plan for success. Think about the following as you begin to craft a business plan for your ageless startup:

- Are you providing a product, a service, or both?
- What business or sector are you going to focus on? Why?
- What problem you are going to solve?
- What kind of potential customers typically have this problem?
- What makes your solution different from others?
- How are you going to make a profit doing this?
- How many customers do you need (and at what price point) to make a profit?
- What expenses will you incur organizing and launching your enterprise?
- What ongoing monthly expenses will you incur after launch?
- How will your customers find you, and how will you find customers?
- Do you have a test market in place to try out your ideas?
- What is your value proposition to your customers? Why should they choose you and your product or service?
- What risks do customers face by doing business with you? How can you minimize those?
- How will your customers know when you've succeeded? What metrics do you use to measure success? For your customers and for yourself?
- What legal form of ownership will you utilize? Why?
- What licenses or permits will you need from regulatory authorities?
- What insurance coverages will be required? What will this cost?
- Do you have an attorney available if needed?
- Who will you use for tax advice and preparation?

Once you answer these questions for yourself, you can build your plan around the outcomes you want to see. That way, you can wall off strategies and outcomes that land you in a place you don't want to be.

As you write your answers down, be short, simple, and direct.

Be tough on yourself. As an ageless startup, you are the first and most important customer. Your plan is your roadmap. And how you answer these initial questions is your first step in creating it.

POSITION YOUR BUSINESS FOR OPTIMAL PLANNING

Before you dive into writing a business plan, set your sights clearly on what you want to accomplish with your ageless startup. Find a specialty that helps specific customers get smarter about their enterprises. Get great at that specialty. Identify a core market of precisely focused end users.

I recommend setting up your enterprise to sell to other businesses. I strongly believe that it's much easier and more rational to make and sell goods or services to other enterprises than to traditional consumers. While your vendors should be as diverse as possible, your customers should be filtered carefully.

> **TIP**
>
> There are many, many enterprises within your reach that could benefit by the addition of smarter, more sustainable business models.

Make one of these models, tools, or processes the thing you're great at. Find a technology niche, a set of tools, or most likely for ageless entrepreneurs, a service you can create inexpensively. Then, target it with skilled accuracy at just the customers you choose.

Ageless startups typically focus on the industries their entrepreneurs grew up in or have special expertise in. Sign up for newsletters from that industry. Connect with leaders of that industry on social media. Attend business conferences in that field. Visit every vendor, and listen for clues about what's coming next. There is no limit to the amount of new information you can continually absorb when it's a field you love. One nugget, one suggestion, one off-hand remark can lead to the next breakthrough for your enterprise.

Breakthroughs don't have to come in extra-large sizes. Breakthroughs usually come in small increments. Breakthroughs are processes done safer and smarter. Breakthroughs can come in all manner of shapes and sizes and levels of recognition. If you can help other enterprises produce their work with less waste, you've got the start of a sustainable business model.

There is a wonderful concept I strongly recommend that focuses on rapidly developing *minimum viable products* (MVPs), which includes service-based businesses. The idea is to create a product or service quickly and (most likely) imperfectly. Perfect is the enemy of the good. The "good" in this case is to get market feedback as you build your business. The old ways of working to roll out a fully conceived and workable small business are no longer viable (if they ever were). Instead, think of how you can go slow, then get bold to launch with confidence. Can you get someone to pay you for something described in your mission, values, and goals? If not, why not? If not, what could you add or subtract from the offer to get someone to buy? This is messy and uncomfortable if you think about it from that perspective. It's helpful and inspiring if you come at it from a different direction.

I come from the helpful direction. Get out fast and learn to fail carefully. Learn the value of "no." How can "no" make you smarter? Sometimes the littlest things make the biggest differences.

I learned this lesson very early, in my first entrepreneurship gig in late grade school. During summers between 6th and 7th grades, and well after 8th grade, I used to ride my bike to the Elmhurst (Illinois) News Agency. We had to get there well before sunrise, with no helmet or lights on the bike, of course.

My regular corner was North Avenue and Route 83 during morning rush hour. I would get off my bike, wait until the light turned red, and then run as fast as I could between the two lanes of cars quickly stacking up, testing what it took to sell papers that morning. Did you show off the paper above the fold as you ran with it through the cars? Did you display the sports section that morning? You could see arms sticking out of car windows through the clouds of 1960s car exhaust, and I would race from arm to arm, selling as many papers as I could until the light changed. I'd then jump through moving traffic, run back to the light, wait for it to change, and then do it again, and again, and again. I got to keep two cents per paper, plus tips. It was fun figuring out how to make chaotic systems work.

It still is.

Quickly get your business offer in place so you can use it to craft your plan. That said, don't plan it to death. Launch it. Learn from it. Improve it. Circle back when the light changes, and do it again. You don't have to run

Ageless Entrepreneur Spotlight

Haywood Fennell Sr., founder of the Oscar Micheaux Family Theater Program and 2007 Purpose Prize Fellow (Massachusetts)

Q: *What did you do as your first career (or your most recent—or all of them)?*

A: My life was a career of blunders for almost half of my life after being discharged with honor from the U.S. military. I was "trapped" in the world of addiction to heroin that introduced me to jails and fails. Even though I would fight to be free of drugs, it was more a physical fight than a spiritual fight with an unwillingness to change my thinking. I had a family and a good wife with then six children that I had left physically but not mentally, as they represented a "rope of hope" that I would not become totally consumed by my lifestyle as a substance abuser with disorders.

Q: *How did you find your current passion? Please share the age when you began your newest work.*

A: I remember being in prison, then around 41 or 42, and many of the inmates could not read nor write, and I began to write missives at their request, trying to get the officials to respond in a favorable way to their requests.

Almost 22 years ago, I was at a Veteran's Administration detox ward kicking a drug habit. I prayed to the Lord to be free of drugs and to write. I founded the Oscar Micheaux Family Theater Program Company here in Boston in 1997 when I was living in a homeless shelter.

Q: *What is the best piece of advice you would share with someone in the second half of life considering entrepreneurship?*

A: Try to be active and stay involved. Do not allow yourself to think that age hinders the thought process. Go for it, and enjoy whatever it is that you feel you can do to be a part of something good. I'm a little over 70, and I'm in it to win it.

between rush hour traffic, but you do have to continually try to sell more and get valuable experience along the way.

CREATE AN AGELESS BUSINESS PLAN

In any kind of organization, especially startups and emerging enterprises, the tectonic plates of what's possible shear up against one another all the time. If you're the leader, the issue of choosing among many good options will end up on your desk. Creating plans in advance to guide future choices based on your mission, values, and goals will simplify those options significantly as they arise.

You need to start early and craft good bones from the start by setting up reliable structures to support the good stuff you can do with your organization: data control, accounting, insurance, legal, logistics. You don't need to spend a fortune. You can start out cheap and easy, but you absolutely need to build your enterprise around good bones for it to be sustainable. Without executing these areas carefully and early in the process, you'll forever be sprinting through your enterprise life, never quite catching up.

TIP

Don't wait for your growth phase to get smart. Never think volume will fix problems. Volume magnifies problems; it does not fix them.

Business plans meet this need. If you haven't written one before, it may seem daunting. But for smaller enterprises, you are writing it for a very valuable audience of one—you. The business plan is there to help YOU—not investors, banks, or business advisors. They may all get to see it at some point, but the ultimate purpose is to help you and your enterprise succeed.

When you're in unknown situations (and there will be many), you can turn to your plan for direction. When you have key choices to make, you'll have your plan to guide you.

When you're launching a new enterprise, no matter how small, the world you are entering can seem chaotic. Opportunities and dangers can look eerily similar. Everything can seem urgent. Your business plan can guide you on the long march to achieve your mission through your values, your goals, and the practices you build around them. With this structure, the urgency falls away and what's important can emerge.

Seth Godin had a great piece in *Fast Company* a while back (April 2004) in which he talked about the misuse of urgency as an excuse when, in fact, it's an indicator that you have put something off until it has no choice but to become an urgent matter.

For example, Godin compares sprinting for your plane instead of doing the harder task of waking up a little earlier. Will you live in drama and chaos, or will you prevent the problem?

This is a nice metaphor for what you need to think about as you approach your startup or grow your emerging enterprise.

Wake up early to the demands that you'll face as an emerging enterprise and a full participant in the global economy. Don't grouse. Get smart.

You need to bulletproof your enterprise to the best of your ability as early as you can. Build in good bones. Accounting, insurance, legal, and data control are boring as hell, done right.

Boring is good. I promise, you do NOT want to see excitement in any one of these areas of your business life. Make your work important, not urgent. That's the core value of any sustainable business plan.

As you work through planning your new enterprise, try to keep in mind a short list of rules of thumb I've used over the years as I have created business plans for myself as an ageless entrepreneur:

▶ *Slow is smarter than fast.* In this case, slow doesn't mean lazy or meandering. It means continuous progress on a pace you can support. Fast typically implies throwing money at something. In business, that's rarely a good solution.

▶ *Embrace the imperfect.* Virtually nothing gets to the "perfect" stage. Show your plans, products, and services to prospective customers early. They will help you refine your ideas and get you to the next steps. Imperfect is an opportunity to do better.

▶ *Be rigorous in capturing data as you plan and as you scale.* As your enterprise grows, the amount of information grows exponentially. You don't just get a new customer; you get phone numbers, email addresses, shipping information, vendor requirements, quotes, orders, and a growing list of important correspondence. How will you capture, store, and retrieve that information?

▶ *Solve real problems that real people experience.* Much of the buzz around entrepreneurship calls for anticipating the next new "hot" product. For ageless entrepreneurs, typically working on their own or in small groups, the core of your entrepreneurial life should revolve around fixing a specific problem that currently exists in the market. Customers for this are already in place.

▶ *Write alternative scripts.* Your first ideas often are not the best. Be ready for unexpected events. As you plan your enterprise, look for alternative ways of routing your new business through the startup maze. I call this "writing scripts." These are not the business plan, but alternatives to the plan you may need down the road. Writing scripts will help you identify where speedbumps may occur. It doesn't cost anything to write scripts. When you need one, you'll be ready.

▶ *It's not sustainable if it's not repeatable.* Any kind of enterprise that has to keep changing its operations to generate needed revenue is not sustainable. The models that you plan, design, and execute need to be predictable and repeatable. It's not sustainable if it's not repeatable. Period.

▶ *Listen more.* Talk less. You don't learn by talking. You don't make progress without learning.

▶ *Failure is just a bump along the learning curve.* You are on a journey. Every journey has pitfalls. Learn from failure and continue, or stay in the pits.

▶ *Create the simplest version (the MVP) of what you want to offer, and test it on model customers.* Get your ideas into the public as soon as you can. Improve. Iterate. Repeat.

▶ *Don't wait for inspiration.* Be the inspiration.

Ageless entrepreneurship is an ideal way to continue to make valuable contributions to your community and the world. Your enterprise life should be one that meets your own mission, values, and goals—and you can show that in your ageless business plan. There are four main areas of the business plan where ageless entrepreneurs can set themselves apart, thanks to the experience they bring to the table: operations and management, marketing, competitive analysis, and financial planning. Let's dig in to each.

Operations and Management

The operations and management of your new enterprise will require your diligence in all areas. Operations and management boil down to creating efficient processes that serve the ultimate goal of providing goods and services to your customers in the most efficient manner possible. This will be your ongoing job. Pay attention.

As you've read, most ageless startups will be run and managed by solo entrepreneurs. This means you'll do as much of the day-to-day business chores (bookkeeping, invoicing, correspondence, etc.) as possible, but that in the end, you will contract with third-party professionals (such as accounting firms) to do the top-level work.

I strongly prefer contracting as many support functions as you can. Hiring employees carries a significant responsibility to oversee and even nurture those people. You'll know when the right time to hire people is upon you.

What is the most import operations management focus for any startup? Sales. Nothing happens until you sell something. You need to build a viable system for managing and operating your company that continuously focuses on getting someone to pay you to solve a problem. That's your operations and management mission.

You get there by building internal systems for accurately—and deeply—capturing the relevant contact information of the people you want to serve. Data capture systems need to not only document the usual who-what-where stuff, but also the 'why' and the relevant conversations that are bringing you and your customers together.

Your operations and management systems as an ageless startup need to focus on getting your MVP into the hands of a small group of real customers as quickly as possible, then improve on that. Over and over. Your future depends on it.

The joy of being an ageless entrepreneur in this circumstance is that you are building the systems for yourself. This is not a sexy slide in an investor pitch deck. This is your plan about how you will make your own life better while you improve the world through your business. Cutting corners works against you. Being unethical or greedy works against you. Working in the short term to the detriment of the future works against you.

Ageless Entrepreneur Spotlight

Lynn Price, founder and president emeritus of Camp To Belong International and 2017 Purpose Prize Fellow (Colorado)

Q: *How did you find your current passion?*

A: Volunteering as a Court Appointed Special Advocate and also at a Child Haven (a children's shelter), I realized I was "one of those kids." Observing and communicating with children in foster care and their care providers, I learned that they weren't confident in anticipating successful futures and siblings were being placed in separate homes. I had defied the odds of foster care failure as I graduated from the University of Illinois followed by family, a successful career, a positive attitude, and a wonderful relationship with my older sister despite our separation.

Q: *What would you do differently now that you've had some time developing your current adventure?*

A: I would have accepted more personal and professional development education around balancing making a living and making a difference—business and passion.

Q: *What is the best piece of advice you would share with someone in the second half of life considering entrepreneurship?*

A: Do it! It is an opportunity to live your passion, be a role-model for your family, make a difference in something meaningful to you, and leave a legacy of caring through action.

What works *for* you? Your own personal integrity, mission, and values should drive your management systems. These are your strongest ageless value propositions to help the world that is coming next.

Market Analysis

A key part of your business plan will be identifying who your target customers are and how you will get to them. You will often hear inexperienced entrepreneurs brag that if they only get a tiny share of the almost unlimited number of people that they will market to, they will be the next big . . . The real finish to that sentence is "failure," because it's an unattainable standard. Selling to a mass market isn't viable for most businesses—especially not for those of us in the artisanal/ageless startup category.

For any entrepreneur, especially ageless solopreneurs, there is not enough time or money in the world to sell to everyone. Marketing takes time and money, and you want to maximize the value of both.

Seth Godin calls this, identifying your minimum viable audience (sort of like your MVP). What is the smallest number of people that can sustain your work? Who would you choose to be in that group? How does your work delight and impress them into choosing you?

I've always believed it was wiser to start businesses that sold services or products to other organizations. It doesn't matter what kind: nonprofit, for-profit, big, small, local, or international.

The main reason for this is economic survival. You can find organizations easier, faster, and cheaper than enough retail sales customers could ever find you. Beyond that, it's much more sustainable, personally and professionally, to work with business-to-business (B2B) transactions.

I acknowledge that sales to consumers are getting easier. You obviously have Amazon, eBay, and the rest. However, I find that doing business on an enterprise-to-enterprise basis is a good way to build a foundation under your new organization. People are directly involved. You learn something vital with every sale. Both sides are looking for reproducible results. If you deliver value, they are glad to pay.

What's nice is that everyone involved in this kind of commerce understands the relationship. They're looking for solutions for their organization, and you, hopefully, have one. You, in turn, use this same model for developing your own support teams both in-house and in your supply chain. Everyone works for the good of each other. This model works if you plan it right.

Organizations that are stuck in their ways are going to stay stuck in their ways. You don't have enough time or money to convince them otherwise.

Organizations that are actively on the hunt and looking for smart, new growth are by necessity looking for valuable new ideas. If you've got a sustainable solution for their organization, prove it. Then round up all similar organizations in that market and make them your target.

> **TIP**
>
> The organizations you need to partner with are searching for smart new ideas and smart, new growth. If you want to be sustainable, customers and market partners with this profile will get you there.

I don't care if it takes a city, county, state, or planet to make up enough potential customers. *That's* your market.

Your target market does not have to be drawn from the hottest, coolest organizations in today's headlines. For most startups and emerging enterprises, you can't afford to play very effectively in that space anyway.

Tom Peters, author of *In Search of Excellence: Lessons from America's Best-Run Companies* (Harper Business, 2006), supports this idea:

> *I also questioned the need to depend on "leading edge" industries. Significant participation in such industries is a plus, no doubt—but once again, it is the excellence of enterprise that matters most. There is, as I see it, almost no such thing as an "old industry"—most every industry is ripe for new approaches.*

Note that carefully, ". . . it is the excellence of enterprise that matters most."

A good solution is a good solution no matter what realm of enterprise you work in. If you can reproducibly fix a real problem, you're launched.

If it's in an out-of-the-way industry or a sector no one is touting, all the better.

As an ageless startup, you have your networks to support you. Your secret weapon is wisdom.

When you find the right customers who understand this value proposition, there is nothing more sustainable than joining hands and racing to the top together. That's your target market.

Competitive Analysis

As ageless entrepreneurs, we have the perspective of what works and what doesn't in commerce. How you identify and deal with competitors will be a key section of your business plan. This is one area of life where it pays to have a grown-up in the room.

Commerce and cooperation are typically touted as opposites. You've heard it—business-as-war stuff: *Grind your opponent down. Drown them in your dust as you speed by. Take no prisoners.*

I don't think so. I see enterprise as the great new global commons. Sure, it's been co-opted from the top down in its early stages, as most good ideas usually are. But successful participation in enterprises of many types is increasingly available to more and more of us, especially ageless entrepreneurs. The commons of global enterprise needs to be defended from the bottom up. That's you and me, doing it right.

Spending your energy on defeating competitors, or worse, denigrating competitors in the public market of your chosen field, is a fool's game. It is always better to look inside yourself first and determine what subsets of the market you excel at. You want your markets to grow, and that means growth for anyone involved that has the chops to keep up with the growth. Market growth means more chances to innovate and to improve the communities and the world we live in. When I enter a new market, I think of competitors as potential partners. What are we both great at? What could we do better together to make our customers stronger and grow the market we all work in, in order to raise the tide for all boats?

TIP

It is a hard enterprise lesson to learn, but cooperation, when justified, is far more efficient than conflict.

Ageless entrepreneurs have the wisdom to know that opportunities come through expanding knowledge and networks. Those are key advantages we have as older startups. Put them to good use.

When you begin your enterprise, you'll be tempted to turn your own personal fears into enterprise fears and react to the world with your fists up. That's not all bad. There are a lot of jerks out there. But it's not all good either.

Life is continuously imperfect, but it's also a world of countless everyday miracles. In your enterprise life, watching trust work and be rewarded is one of those everyday miracles—not just on the personal level, but more so in the ways it builds and grows the public commons for all of us.

If you want to succeed on any enterprise path, look for ways to cooperate with your enterprise partners rather than battling with them. The goal is to create ever-increasing value for the solutions you provide. This means involving customers, vendors, peers, investors, community members, and everyone in between as part of this trust thing.

Sure, you always need to remember the good fences/good neighbors rule. That helps spot the bad actors who don't share your community-based vision sooner. Let them fall away. The good ones will reward you with the small miracles, the pathways, and the tools of your ageless startup.

Life is an unbroken series of collaborations with strangers. We collaborate hundreds of times each day with people we don't know while driving cars. We collaborate with strangers while grocery shopping, at sporting events, taking mass transit, and in dozens of other public interactions.

Your business life can model this. You shouldn't care what the motivation of competitors is. You should know where the lanes are and how everyone should use them. You can change lanes on your own, of course, but the goal is to be a better driver yourself rather than to pass everyone else on the road. Your enterprise life may be geared toward nonprofit work, social entrepreneurship, or your own business. In every circumstance, you'll need friends more than you'll need enemies.

Don't worry about roadblocks or competitors. Work on creating ever-increasing value with your own work. Work to provide ever-better relationships every day. Outwork and outshine lesser competitors and less valuable solutions.

Then, keep your powder dry and trust those who earn your respect. It's the only path I know to planning a successful ageless startup.

Ageless Entrepreneur Spotlight

Sister Marilyn Lacey, founder and executive director of
Mercy Beyond Borders (California)

Q: *What did you do as your first career (or your most recent - or all of them)?*

A: Over my 50 years as a Catholic sister, I've morphed from high school math teacher to overseas refugee camp worker to refugee resettlement manager in the U.S. to founder and executive director of the nonprofit Mercy Beyond Borders (MBB).

Q: *What would you do differently now that you've had some time developing your current adventure?*

A: I would have spent more time developing back office systems for data collection and program evaluation before jumping in to start projects overseas. I would have worked harder at reaching out to other organizations to seek viable partnerships. I would have been more strategic about forming our board of directors.

Q: *Are there any mistakes you can share from your own current career?*

A: Oh, too many to count. The biggest obstacle to being effective in other cultures is the blindness we all have toward our own cultural biases and ways of looking at the world. No one wants to be the "ugly American," and yet sometimes we blunder in, unconsciously assuming we know best how to do things.

Financials

The reason you set up and maintain professional accounting systems is to monitor all aspects of your enterprise financial life. But the short course in this is cash flow management. Rule number one is to bring in more than you spend—and that's something you will need to show in your business plan.

If you are going to launch an ageless startup by bootstrapping—which I recommend—cash is everything. It's a simple, yet powerful way to see if your business is growing or stalled.

Your ageless startup should not be relied upon to pay your personal bills in the early stages. You are launching a new model that will take time to establish. Your goal for your new model is sustainability.

There are only three key things you need to focus on to keep your enterprise sustainable. Most of us who've been through startups a few times will tell you we've screwed up and lost, or nearly lost, everything because of these three key things. If somebody tells you they've been through startups and haven't screwed up one of these three key issues, they're lying.

Ready?

The three key things for sustaining your business: Cash flow. Cash flow. Cash flow.

This means available cash. This means money to pay the business bills and money to invest in the next project, to grow your enterprise wisely. Everything else in your business can be hitting on all cylinders, but if cash flow goes bad, you're out of the pool.

This should be fairly straightforward for ageless startups.

You need to keep a sufficient reserve of cash on hand to pay all your obligations promptly. The only way to do this on your own is to keep enough work (and invoices) in the pipeline to keep refilling your business bank account. Banks and investors don't wait until you have sufficient funds to pay them their due. You should treat yourself the same way. Make sure your cash flow is sufficient to meet your bills with enough left over to pay yourself.

While this sounds onerous, the options can be even more difficult. Taking out loans to meet expenses can mask the reality of the health of your business. Loans and investments are needed in high-growth venture startups, but for one person or small ageless startups, those metrics need not apply.

The Bootstrap Method

Among the greatest values of an ageless startup is that they can be started with very little money using the do-it-yourself (DIY) approach you read about in Chapter 2 called *bootstrapping*. You put your own small amount of money in first. Then you grow your company with the profits from each sale. This is a slow process, but it bakes in the notion that each job you take requires that you make a profit. Otherwise, you are going backwards, and it will be much harder to make up with the next job. You should write your business plan accordingly and bake your bootstrapping approach into it.

Using a bootstrapping approach doesn't mean that you won't eventually seek and secure outside funding; it just means that you are leveraging your financial risk early using seed money. This is used to wire up the organization and bring it to life. Depending on registrations, licenses, and insurance, you should be able to fund your launch yourself with a thousand dollars or so of seed money, perhaps even less.

At the stage where your business begins to grow, you will be tempted to reach out for outside investors. If you build a model that requires outside funding, you are putting yourself at a significant disadvantage. At this stage, you can rule out venture capital or even angel investors. Outside money for small startups comes almost exclusively from the "Three F's": family, friends, and fools. This seems like a no-brainer at first, but think about sharing your life with crazy nephew Carbuncle last Thanksgiving or having that friend from the neighborhood demanding everything from price breaks to free stuff from your new business. It's just not worth it.

Bootstrapping is the ideal way to launch an ageless startup. If you decide to grow something big down the road, you will be in good bootstrapping territory with companies like Cisco, Microsoft, and eBay that had their origins rooted in bootstrapping.

This is not a rant against venture funding. Those kinds of firms can also be quite valuable. But many of those leaders are keenly aware of the risks that outside funding can create.

If small businesses can learn to launch and grow using their own money, without having to change their business models to meet the demands of outside funding, they can flourish at a smaller scale that supports themselves, their families, and their communities. These entrepreneurs will in large part be able to control their own destinies, while the world will benefit from their innovations and hard work.

Bootstrapping is not a code for unprofessionalism. Just the opposite. You have to run your business as though you and your community depended on it. Use your bootstrapping phase to get smart, make mistakes, and build a market. It will take more time but less money than you think. Use your financial documents in your business plan to chart your course and to give you a map to check against as you travel into the future.

Self-enterprise is a path to personal independence and growing vibrant communities. But for most new enterprises, that journey needs to be one of bootstrapping, self-funding, and longer timelines than you expect. You should build all of these factors into your business plan.

As you've read, ageless startups are typically operated by a solo entrepreneur. Under these circumstances, your business bank account and the statements it generates will be your guiding star for cash management as you create the business plan (and thereafter). When setting up your business checking account, look for financial institutions with excellent online access and tools. Everyone is offering these, but some are much better than others. I have found some of the best of these at local credit unions, rather than at the national banks. In almost all cases, the ability to rapidly check on your financial status online and communicate with the financial institution easily are key to efficiency.

Before you create your plan, visit with the person or company that will act as your CPA or financial manager. The first document you want them to help you prepare is your *chart of accounts*. This is a very basic document identifying all the specific areas where you anticipate spending money (insurance, travel, office supplies, etc.) and receiving money (usually from just one or a few sources initially, depending on your enterprise).

You can fill these out monthly and over time aggregate the numbers to give yourself a snapshot of how and where money arrives and leaves.

Good management here will also be key to efficient tax preparation in your early years.

You will also want to prepare a startup budget for your new enterprise. This is the roadmap for how much money you will need to invest in your startup as well as how and when you expect to see money coming in.

This is your estimate of what you'll need on hand to open your business and how much it will cost to operate initially. If you are following a slow startup model, you can add these startup costs over time, as funds are available, and you can reflect that in your business plan.

As a new entrepreneur, it will be best to overestimate your startup costs and underestimate how much revenue will be coming in initially. The goal is to never outrun your cash available. If you use a small amount of personal debt initially, do not consider that a trap door you can keep escaping into. The goal is to get a positive cash flow underway as soon as possible, with the smallest reasonable (to you) amount of expense invested. Then the focus for solo entrepreneurs is to take in more than you spend.

Financial Statements

Beyond these as your business plan starts to take shape, you will want to learn about cash flow statements and income statements, also known as profit and loss statements (P&Ls). Your accounting firm can help you prepare these for your plan, but you should also utilize the many free resources available for understanding these documents (noted in the resources section at the end of the book).

A *cash flow statement* (CFS) is part of a larger financial report that you and your financial professionals will begin generating as your business grows in complexity. In short, the CFS identifies where your funds are coming from, where they go, and how available cash is impacted by the other parts of your business financials, such as inventory. The CFS will become a key part of your overall business financial statement along with the balance sheet and income or profit and loss statement.

A *balance sheet* is simply a statement that details your assets and liabilities. An *income statement*, or *profit and loss statement* (P&L), is a financial report identifying the full range of revenues, costs, and expenses during a specific time period, usually quarterly. As your business grows,

Ageless Entrepreneur Spotlight

Gary Eichhorn, founder, CEO, and board chair of Music & Youth Initiative
and 2017 Purpose Prize Fellow (Massachusetts)

Q: *What is your advice for others considering entrepreneurship?*

A: Why not use our expertise in building collaborative partnerships in the for-profit world to strengthen nonprofit organizations rather than trying to recreate the wheel? Building partnerships was a key part of my professional career. While I worked at HP, for example, I developed partnerships with our competitors including Microsoft and IBM. I saw the power and the leverage of partnerships in the business world and was anxious to put the same principles to work in the nonprofit sector.

My advice to others is to find your passion and leverage your strengths. For those who have been successful businesspeople, I would not underestimate how different the nonprofit world is. Yes, there are skills to be leveraged, but it is important to be humble and willing to partner and learn from those who have been serving in their community for many years. They will welcome your contribution if you respect theirs.

Be bold. Be passionate. Take risks. Expect to learn from everyone around you. There is no reason to fear anything or anyone. Trying is much more important than succeeding. Assume that others want to help you do good. Spread joy wherever you go. It's contagious!

Q: *How did you grow your new organization?*

A: We could have created a music school for underserved youth and reached tens of young people, but there are millions of kids who would love to have music in their lives. We knew we could never reach them all, but we wanted to try. So our approach is focused on two key objectives: leverage and sustainability. We collaborate with already successful youth development organizations. Through a rigorous five-year program, they learn how to sustain a high quality afterschool music program that they own. We "teach them to fish." As they say, give me a lever, and I will move the world.

you may find the need to prepare more complex and detailed financial reports for your business plan. The purpose of these will be to back up your plan with hard numbers to demonstrate to banks or investors to prove your model. This is a document that utilizes your startup budget and estimated income for the coming year. This is a good report card for you to check your progress against. It is a good tool for forecasting and paying your estimated taxes to the IRS.

In the excitement of launching a startup, creating financial reporting documents may not be at the top of your list. But putting clear and meaningful projections and financial reports in place, even for the smallest businesses, can help you navigate all that startup excitement and come out whole, as well as profitable, after you launch.

So, as you launch, keep great records of every step, starting in your business plan. While this is typically not the fun part for most of us, having effective financial records to support your business is the basis for having fun as your enterprise grows.

SHOWCASE YOUR NICHE

Your business plan should celebrate the small niche you are in. You should not apologize to yourself or anyone else for a tightly focused sales market. It is a remarkable advantage, one that can energize your sales and marketing efforts by keeping you dedicated to your mission, values, and goals.

Consider my friend and ageless entrepreneur Joan Beverley Izzo, interviewed in this book. Joan is a remarkable seamstress who has taken her talents into a seemingly miniscule (to most of the rest of us) niche. She helps families repurpose treasured family fabrics like a great-grandmother's wedding dress, mom's christening gown, and grandfather's beloved ties. These fabrics as a whole are often fragile and deteriorating. Joan saves what is useable and creates new, more resilient family heirlooms for the families to use while creating new ways for people to remember, honor, and celebrate their ancestors.

This seems like such a tiny niche, yet by focusing on those potential customers that match her business, her mission, and her values, Joan has a long waiting list and is one of the more successful ageless entrepreneurs I know.

How do you go about finding and showcasing your niche in your business plan? Start with making a list just for yourself. What you know and what you love will be what carries you the furthest in your new enterprise, so start with what's in your heart. Do NOT start with what can make money. That will follow. As you create your business plan, ask yourself:

▶ What problems do you see in the world you can help solve?

▶ What subject area, no matter how small, are you drawn to in your own life?

▶ What were you good at in your past work?

▶ What were the hard parts of that work that others avoided?

▶ When researching subjects of interest to you, where do you wish you'd see better information? What's missing? Where can you add to the story?

▶ Are there ideas you love that big businesses can't or don't serve any longer?

▶ What words best describe your niche? Searching for all the key-words that describes your subject will help define the scope of the opportunity.

▶ List the companies serving your intended market. Identify their strengths and weaknesses.

▶ Close your eyes and imagine your ideal customer. Try to see them in as much detail as you can. Try to imagine them facing the problems you intend to solve. What are their current options?

▶ Get yourself in front of likely customers and see if your ideas resonate.

▶ Are there related problems to the one you are focusing on? Can you solve several issues by capturing the trust and commerce of your target customer?

▶ Find the vendors serving your intended market. What does their marketing focus on?

▶ Begin building your network of like-minded people within your niche. Go slow and find collaborators you might partner with to grow commerce for all involved.

▶ What can you learn from existing commerce within your niche? Who are the players? What are they missing? What kind of customers are they focusing on? What price points are they selling their products and services at? What kinds of customers can't they serve? Why can't they serve them? How can you organize a system to serve the underserved?

▶ Reach out to strangers associated with your potential niche and ask for an opportunity to discuss or to advise.

▶ Begin to research potential names and web addresses for your business. You can start with any search engine to search specific web addresses (URLs). When you find active sites using your idea, research them carefully. What can you learn? What is missing? What can you do better, smarter, faster, and in a better value proposition for the customer?

As startups and emerging enterprises, we all can benefit from this newly emerging niche business model. A niche market is not a small collection of customers. A niche market is a community of like-minded people who share a passion or an idea that has great meaning to them. Niche marketing is a service to a community you also are passionate about, delivered with wisdom, humility, and professional excellence. By focusing on individuals and their specific needs, you can solve real problems and make a difference in their lives. It's a much more sustainable business strategy. It's better to be a hero to a small number of people who will in turn promote you to their friends, than to scream into howling winds of big consumer markets where no one can hear you, much less care what you have to say. For the ageless entrepreneur, niche markets are the perfect home.

CREATE A PLAN B

I've been holding fast to a quote by James Yorke, a mathematician and scholar, who coined the term and propelled the field of chaos theory. *Chaos theory* is often summarized as butterflies flapping their little wings on the other side of the world, leading to unpredictable outcomes such as big weather changes elsewhere.

That idea is used to illuminate a central tenant of chaos theory, the idea that an act so small, so distant, so seemingly random and irrelevant can have monstrous, life- and universe-changing consequences. The theory applies to more than just the weather; it can be used to explain the course of history, interplanetary gravitational pulls, and yes, even our own messy lives.

It's not my point here that you'll be facing chaos in your enterprise life. That's a given. You're hopefully doing something new, fixing

Ageless Entrepreneur Spotlight

Peter Samuelson, film producer, philanthropist, cofounder, president, and
CEO of Starlight Children's Foundation, Starbright World, First Star,
EDAR (Everyone Deserves A Roof), ASPIRE (Academy for Social Purpose
in Responsible Entertainment) and 2015 Purpose Prize Fellow (California)

Q: *What is the best piece of advice you would share with someone considering entrepreneurship?*

A: The first thing I say is, "Don't fuss around initially with planning to put one foot in front of the other. Forget planning first steps. Go and sit in the garden with a yellow pad or the electronic equivalent. Half-close your eyes and try to imagine that it's five or 10 years from now—long enough that your whole amazing idea has actually already happened. Don't worry about raising the money—you've already raised the money. You've already staffed it. You've gone through 22 business plans. Just imagine that it's already done.

What is it that you are dreaming of? Flesh out your dream. What does it look like? Who is there? Who are the clients, the customers? What do they get? Why did they come? What do they get out of it? Who are the staff? What does the product or service do? Why is it terrific? Write it down on your yellow pad, or put it in your digital whatever. Then edit it and edit it and edit it. That is your goal in two to five pages.

Don't worry about how to get there initially; just describe it to yourself. You'll find that your imagination fills in some blanks. Once you've done that, you've established your goals. It's a whole heck of a lot easier to then say to yourself, "What would exist at the halfway point between now and then? What would be the best kind of armature for the clay sculpture?" And then it's easier to come back to the quarter-way point and say, "If we were headed for that kind of success, what would the first version of it look like? What would be the low-hanging fruit?" Then, you can come backwards much more easily from that point and start saying, "We have to have some employees; we have to pay rent; what's the budget," and this and that. Then, it becomes easy to come back from that budget—not just a money budget, but a people budget—it's easier than to reverse-engineer than to say, "Now let's get back to the very beginning with me sitting here in the garden."

Just go straight to what success looks like. If you completely understand what success looks like, it's much easier to go backwards towards what would be the beginning to create that success. And then what would be the beginning of *that* beginning? This process eventually gets all the way back to the beginning, and not only that, but you've already worked out how to pitch it because you lived it.

Q: *What are the most common mistakes entrepreneurs make?*

A: Would-be entrepreneurs—the ones who fail—think they need to know how to do everything themselves. When I make a film, I'm not a scriptwriter. I'm not a cinematographer. I don't direct. I can't act. I'm not an art director or a production designer. I'm not a sound recorder or a story editor. I'm not a publicist, or any of those hundred jobs that there are on a film. I just know how to hire them.

Q: *Any advice for learning new subject areas?*

A: Apprenticeship is important. It's important for someone to say, "I don't know how to do this. Why don't I go and offer to someone who is doing something a little bit similar; can I shadow them for a month? Can I watch how you do it? And I'll just be the silent listener in the room. But I'll go to all your meetings with you." After someone's been to a hundred meetings, they pretty much know a whole lot that they would never have gotten from a lecture in an MBA class. So, apprenticeship, I think, is a helpful thing.

problems, and generating new economic geographies. Chaos comes with the territory. Keep at it.

What I'd like to emphasize is the randomness of the universe and your enterprise. While you're in the midst of everything that you will face, nothing can be taken as certain. Absolute certainties sometimes fail. Sure things often aren't.

Don't get me wrong. Getting as close as you can to certain and sure is the gold standard metric. Push, try, refine, and get closer continuously. But most of the time, life happens. Obscure events can send waves through your enterprise life that defy logic but do, in fact, occur in spite of your best efforts.

Dr. Yorke, among the most acknowledged and rewarded minds of our time, summed up this position deftly in a quote from *New Scientist Magazine* in 2005. I'd like to suggest it as a core value of your ageless entrepreneur life. It's as close to true as anything I know about sustainable work.

The most successful people are those who are good at Plan B.

You need to move to be able to jettison all or parts of Plan A when the evidence dictates. The key to having an effective Plan B is to be continuously building it.

Entrepreneurs should always have a Plan B in progress. No plan is perfect. Great plans evolve. Plan Bs rarely include wholesale changes to your mission, values, and goals. The changes are iterative and added in small steps.

How do you do this? Carefully. Successful entrepreneurs don't change with every "no" they get, but they do listen and watch carefully as their product or service navigates its early first steps in the market. When enough evidence accumulates that you may need to adjust your plan, you can test and implement those changes as appropriate.

After successful sales or contracts, ask your customers what you could have done better, what more they would like to have seen from your work, and what didn't meet their expectations.

After unsuccessful proposals, ask what the prospect thought was missing from your offer.

As you accumulate more and more of these responses, you'll get a good sense of where your plan is working and where it needs to be changed.

Often, these suggestions from customers can grow into significant new plans for your business.

Stay closely connected to industry news for the kind of products or services you are providing. Follow industry leaders online. Subscribe to the best industry newsletters. Read the blogs of thought leaders in your field. As you grow in confidence and knowledge, you'll begin to develop alternative ideas for your business plan. The key to having a great Plan B is to always be building it.

Earlier in the chapter, we discussed writing alternative scripts for your business plan. First ideas are often not the best ones. New information emerges. Problems arise. Opportunities develop as your enterprise matures. This is not theoretical. This is probable. Your own Plan B is a way of acknowledging that your business plan is flexible enough to meet the challenges and opportunities in a changing market. What happens if your social media strategy doesn't work? What happens if customers don't buy at the price point you anticipated? Your Plan B can be a series of scripts that explore what happens when the unexpected occurs and predictions in your plan don't come true. You will likely not need many of these, but the ones you do need will be waiting for you. And you will be grateful that your business Plan B components were in place.

PUT YOUR BUSINESS PLAN TO WORK

Once you have your plan secure, it's time to take it on the road and use it to find support. As I mentioned earlier, bootstrapping your ageless startup at first is a smart move, so your first task with the finished business plan isn't necessarily to seek monetary support but to seek other kinds of support. While many programs are set up to help you find third-party financing, your road to success doesn't start there. I believe ageless startups need to first flesh out their markets and get cash flow moving on its own. It doesn't have to be huge, but you need to prove your market first. Without that, all the startup funding you could ever locate won't matter.

Look for Assistance Programs

I suggest you look first to assistance programs that offer advice and mentoring. There are wonderful public and private organizations everywhere promoting and supporting the world of emerging enterprises. This level of support is typically free or readily available.

TIP

Do your homework. Get your feet wet. First look to the support organizations that can help your planning skills. They're out there.

Finding free programs to assist your business development is not hard. Nearly every technical school, college, and university will have programs to assist entrepreneurs in their communities, be they rural or urban or everything in between. Typically, you can find these assistance programs by searching for "entrepreneurship" or "small business" on their websites or using a search engine with these terms and the name of the school. Call them up and find out how to learn more. Join their mailing lists. Search out their social media sites and follow their work.

Be a Student . . . Again

Academic institutions often have business accelerator programs you can join for free or for a modest cost. These programs will take you through the business startup process from A to Z. Often, there is a pitch competition at the end of these where accelerator members pitch a group of investors for investments. Others offer prize money (typically modest) for various levels of success. For ageless entrepreneurs, the pitch to investors, even the prize money, is not important. It's the real-time reviews and feedback for your business model that you receive by going through the process.

Academic institutions with advance business degrees will commonly have programs to offer analysis by MBA students of your business concepts and plans. I just helped a young entrepreneur enter one of these programs at a local university, and he had 20 MBA students doing analytical work on everything from his finances, to marketing, to sales and distribution—at no cost to the entrepreneur.

Because academic organizations are chartered to provide a public service, many of these business programs and courses are online, often at no charge or a small fee. This is the kind of support most entrepreneurs can only dream of. But with your plan in place, you can find it.

A bonus is that you, as an ageless entrepreneur, are respectfully referred to as a non-traditional student. Non-traditional students are among the hottest commodities being sought after in this sector. The demographics of our country are rapidly changing. There are now well over 100 million of us in the second half of life, and younger students are not coming into the academic systems in numbers they once did.

For example, a reference for a technical college program is the Small Business Certificate at the Waukesha County Technical College in Wisconsin. I supported this program as it was being developed. There will be many other similar programs in areas near you, though the online learning community has many similar offerings available.

Go with the Government

There are also many wonderful programs offered through local, county, and state governments. It is often smartest to call your own local municipality first or search their websites for small-business assistance. If they do not operate business assistance programs themselves, they will know where to find them. County governments often have economic development offices. These organizations will have lists of small business development and assistance programs in their regions. I find this to be a good level to do research at because the county-level folks will have information about programs at the municipal and academic levels in their region but will also be connected to state and national level programs available to you. Don't be shy. Call them. It's their job.

The Small Business Administration (SBA) and Service Corps of Retired Executives (SCORE) both have a wealth of information available online that you can utilize, as well as offices throughout the U.S. The SBA has a good online information site called 10 Steps to Start Your Business (https://www.sba.gov/business-guide/10-steps-start-your-business/).

You can drill down into every one of the steps to learn in greater detail. They also have a great resource locator for finding business assistance in your own community at https://www.sba.gov/local-assistance/find/.

SCORE is a resource partner of SBA. They have many offices across the U.S., each with different levels of support and education. A core function they all support is the ability to pair you with an appropriate business mentor at no charge. In an earlier business, I was paired with a mentor who became a lifelong friend and honored resource in my life. You can find your closest SCORE office here: https://www.score.org/.

As an ageless entrepreneur, you are in the driver's seat. There are many programs available for free or modest cost to help you design, build, and grow your business.

Take advantage of these opportunities. Nothing else will come this easy in your business life.

CHAPTER 5 DELIVERABLES

Creating business plans for ageless startups is an exercise that should be designed for you and your target market, nobody else. Your goal is to get paid for fixing problems. Every business decision you make should keep this plan in focus. Your experiences, both failures and successes, will inform this journey. Learn to share your story. Learn to collaborate. Practice transparency and ethics. All of these actions will help you craft a better business plan. Business plans for ageless entrepreneurs should be carefully crafted roadmaps for making you a better businessperson and the world a better place. Remember:

- ▶ *Your expertise is your currency.* Let your own knowledge and strengths guide your plans.
- ▶ *Find the problems.* Look for what's missing in the market and create a plan to help position your startup as the answer to those problems.
- ▶ *Breakthroughs come in small increments.* Your business plan should reflect that by providing specific details about each small step to scaling your startup.
- ▶ *Boring is good.* You don't have to be the flashiest business in your industry. Sometimes, solving the boring problems is a better long-term strategy for growth.
- ▶ *Collaborate or fail.* Your business has several stakeholders, so keep them in mind as you craft your plan. Even better, rely on their input as you are writing it.

▶ *Showcase your niche.* There are many opportunities in smaller niche markets. Make sure your plan reflects that.

▶ *Always keep building your Plan B.* Your business plan should be agile enough to help you map out alternate routes to success.

▶ *Cashflow. Cashflow. Cashflow.* Get your financial documents in order to tell the story of how you plan to maximize cashflow and profit margins.

If your plan is the living document that tells the story of your ageless startup, then the systems you use to run the day-to-day operations are your insurance policy to ensure that things run smoothly. That's what we'll cover in the next chapter.

MAKING SURE YOUR STARTUP IS SYSTEM-SECURE

I keep feeling a need to write about the blue-sky stuff swirling around startups. That part is so fun and so beguiling. I can't wait. However, I also hear the cartoon "good" angel whispering in my other ear, over and over, "Good bones first. Good bones first."

If you don't build in good bones from the outset (a solid structure to support your enterprise), you can quickly drown in blue-sky dreams. For the ageless entrepreneur, those good bones come in the form of reliable systems that work for you in a sustainable way—not ones that you have to micromanage on a daily basis. What, exactly, does a sustainable enterprise look like? "Sustainable" means being able to quickly get to purchase orders, invoices, and contact info for some screwed up job from three years ago with someone from that company on the phone mad at you about who knows what. Sustainable means having those documents available to prove your point and cover your backside.

Not very glamorous, is it? You don't need glamour. You need sustainability. You need systems you can rely on for the long term.

Here's an example from my days at Banner Graphics. Back then, I eventually found that I needed a different product mix than the one I'd started with. I identified signs and banners as a good potential market and created the tools to do that kind of printing. After a month or so of testing the printing systems, I made up some samples and set off on my bicycle to introduce this wondrous new service to retailers in my hometown. I started with the little retail district near my home where I had grown up with some of the proprietors. Somehow, none of them signed up to buy anything. I couldn't figure it out. I went to a nearby retail district but got the same results. I decided to tackle the downtown shopping district. I started at one end and visited every retail store on the main street. One after another turned me down. I didn't know why. I felt so bad that all I wanted to do was get out of their store and move to the next one. It soon became clear that I was running out of businesses to call on. As I got to the end of Main Street, I was down to the last few businesses, one of which was a record shop.

 Ageless Entrepreneur Spotlight

Reid Cox, cofounder of iFoster and 2017 Purpose Prize Fellow (California)

Q: *What did you do as your first career?*

A: My professional background was primarily finance and financial communications. I started consulting to pre-IPO companies as they were looking to go public and start their messaging and introductions to the financial community. As iFoster gained traction and consumed more time, I gradually reduced consulting to focus on my new encore career.

Q: *How did you find your current passion?*

A: My wife spent time in foster care, and that experience created a very personal motivation for us to help foster kids and their caregivers. We spent years discussing the needs of those in foster care and how our careers might apply. So we created iFoster, and it has since become the largest national online community in foster care with members in all 50 states. We bridge the two worlds we lived in, the foster care system and the corporate world, to bring new resources and opportunities into our community to give our children and youth a better chance to reach their potential.

Q: *Are there any mistakes you can share from your own current career?*

A: I think the key concept here is that failing doesn't help anyone, so at the risk of sounding flippant, do what you can to avoid failing, even if it means tapping the brakes occasionally, stopping something you started because it isn't making sense, passing on an opportunity because it takes you down a questionable path, or not listening to your customers. I think we've made all of these mistakes (except not listening to your customers) in our enthusiasm and conviction. Time-to-market pressure applies to social enterprises as much as it does to for-profit startups, but instead of capturing market share, the risk is not helping your market as soon and as much as you want to.

Q: *What is the best piece of advice you would share with someone in the second half of life considering entrepreneurship?*

A: Life deals you opportunities to be the person you want to be; take advantage of them when they come up. Pay attention to the path you are following in life. What experiences, interests, and skills you are accumulating; how you love to spend your free time; what do you find rewarding? And when opportunities come up that combine them, jump at them. You may find that one opportunity leads to another, and another, and you start filling up more of your life with your individual purpose, and you find the entrepreneurial opportunities to start or improve the thing that you are uniquely capable of contributing the most to. That's the beauty of an encore career: life has taught you so much that you now have to give back.

The record store owner heard me out but said no, he didn't need my signs. This time I asked why not. He told me that business was down, and he was restricted to doing promotions only once a month, and I was there at the wrong time. I asked why business was down and he shared his best guesses. I wrote every bit of that down as we talked. It occurred to me that his promotion plan needed a boost and that my services could help. I offered to make him a free sample if he'd sign up for a regular purchasing program with my new company. We agreed to the experiment.

In exchange for the free sample I'd offered, the owner traded me my choice of a free album from the discount bins at the back of the store. I carefully selected a jazz album by Miles Davis. I treasured that album for decades, eventually wearing out the vinyl it was recorded on.

I remember the album, but the most memorable event from that transaction was learning to capture and analyze the customer information. All I really had to do was get out of my own skin and listen to the customer. What did they need? Why did they need it? How could I craft up an offer that met those needs? How was I going to save that information? How could I look up that information month after month, year after year to make sure I was serving their needs? How could I keep that information in a format that I could easily and accurately get into my accounting? How would I save and retrieve the little sidebar notes that informed my understanding of how this customer approached their business? The importance of creating those systems has stayed with me for a lifetime. I still dial up the Miles Davis when I need some great music to accompany my time capturing business data of the day. In this chapter, I'll walk you through some of the systems you need to have in place to make your ageless startup secure for the long term.

GOOD BONES

In my opinion, you shouldn't even start your ageless enterprise until you get the following things underway. It doesn't cost you anything to get smart. There are low-cost entry points for all the following subject areas. You just need to find the pieces that fit you and your budget.

ACCOUNTING

You need to talk to a few CPA offices before you start and present the case for your enterprise and how much of it you want to do under their supervision. Ask if they want to be involved and how much it's going to cost. The CPA won't do your books. You will do the books initially, and you'll be supported as needed by one of their lower-level employees. They will provide solid, independent expertise you don't have. Good CPA outfits would be wise to have some kind of free startup tools available for this situation.

Others will disagree, but I believe even the smallest enterprises need numbers that are certifiable by outsiders for those numbers to be worth a damn. It's not a cost to you; it's a benefit to you. It's a necessity for your business. You can trust the numbers and sleep better at night knowing you haven't blown something important inadvertently. Unless of course, you really love reading business and tax law.

Sometime in the future, you're going to need to present numbers certified by third-party accountants. You'll need to show your numbers to people so they can understand your business situation: bankers, investors, grant agencies, etc.

Start now. Start early when there are no problems of retrofitting your accounting data into yet another software program. Retrofitting accounting systems beautifully illustrates the famous task of stuffing 10 pounds of stuff into a five-pound bag.

Once you get your accounting protocols in place, it becomes easy background noise for the fun stuff ahead. Without those protocols in place, I hope you're feeling lucky.

INSURANCE

You need business liability protection. It's not expensive. You can add bigger umbrella coverage cheaply. Yes, it's a cost, but you get to sleep at night. That's my kind of benefit.

It doesn't matter how simple your enterprise is. Get the insurance. Talk to several agents. Get quotes from an agent you like. They're businesspeople, too. They need to do their best for you to keep themselves sustainable. Good ones will explain carefully what each part of their policy does for you. Most small startups will need coverage for general liability, and most startups (my kind anyway) don't typically have much physical property involved so the costs of that portion should be cheap.

Personal health insurance is another subject for a separate discussion. That's the 500-pound gorilla in the corner for small startups. Startups need access to healthcare to support entrepreneurship. Period.

You can research health care options through groups like AARP (www.aarp.org). At the national level, you can explore insurance alternatives at the website Healthcare.gov (www.healthcare.gov). Individual states can have health insurance plans available. Find out more by calling your state insurance office. If you had access to a health plan through a former employer or through your spouse, you can continue that coverage through COBRA for up to an additional 36 months depending on your own details. To research your COBRA options, you can also visit the COBRA section of the Healthcare.gov site (https://www.healthcare.gov/unemployed/cobra-coverage/). If you are eligible for Medicare, there are also many plans available to fit specific needs.

CLIENT DATA MANAGEMENT

You can start with pencils and notebooks, but you'll need to go digital as soon as possible. There are many tools and approaches to the problem of creating a data management system, and we'll parse them out in time here. For now, try to anticipate every separate data point that you can think of. Build systems to capture and store that data in ways that can be searched and retrieved on demand. If you're smart about designing your data management systems, the value of your data will continue to enhance and grow your enterprise.

You need to start by capturing contact information and relevant notes from viable contacts (an idea you first read about in Chapter 3). Viable contacts are people you meet in your enterprise life that have a reasonable chance of becoming a customer or a valued stakeholder of some kind. If it is someone just bouncing off your work like a skipping stone, you don't have to capture their data. Let them prove you wrong when they come back with something more relevant.

For those you want to keep in your data file, I capture this information in separate searchable fields:

- Organization name
- First name
- Last name
- Job title
- Organization address
- Contact office telephone number
- Contact mobile phone number
- Contact email
- Organization web site
- Organization social sites
- Date/time stamped space for storing key correspondence
- All quotes you have prepared for this contact
- All job-related notes for each quote
- All orders received from this contact
- All job-related notes for each order

There are many other small fields I use to store less important data and ways to search my files, but these are the major ones to keep available for the life of your enterprise.

I prefer databases for this task. You can build a system that matches your needs. Most important, your data storage method needs to be quickly searchable.

I use an off-the-shelf database system that is written for civilians to program/customize. I wrote a simple, searchable database that captures and connects the list of key contact information, quotes, and orders listed above. The mission is self-protection. Who said what, when, and why? The key is to make all these details interconnected and immediately searchable. I've

TIP

Simple, basic, bulletproof data control is essential. The blue sky stuff is important of course, but without data and document mastery in place, that blue sky stuff gets cloudy fast.

found databases to be an ideal platform for this kind of work. Spreadsheets have their place, but they are not designed to hold the deep historical information that entrepreneurship requires.

 Ageless Entrepreneur Spotlight

Annie Griffiths, founder and executive director of Ripple Effect Images and 2017 Purpose Prize Fellow (Virginia)

Q: *What did you do as your first career?*

A: I went straight from being a waitress to being a photographer and started work at *National Geographic* in 1978.

Q: *How did you find your current passion?*

A: In my work with *National Geographic*, I had the opportunity to spend time with women in dozens of countries and realized that their stories were rarely told. They were often misrepresented in western media only as victims, not as the survivors and leaders in their communities that they truly are.

Q: *Are there any mistakes you can share from your own current career?*

A: The learning curve in starting a nonprofit is huge. I have made many mistakes and have counted on the support advice of many individuals who helped me course-correct and grow in my role. I was also helped by what I learned from women in the developing world about collaboration and determination.

Q: *What is the best piece of advice you would share with someone in the second half of life considering entrepreneurship?*

A: I think it's important to examine honestly how much impact they can have; is there a real need for the new endeavor, or is there an existing entity that could use their help?

If you want your business to be sustainable, you need smart, rugged data control systems in place from the start. That's the basis of building a great practice.

BANKING

A little secret here: As a small startup, you're not really big enough for banks to care about. Sorry to break it to you. As long as you're not expecting too much, banks have a lot of good perks for small startups. Look carefully for a simple, easy-to-use online banking interface with things like online bill pay (only the bank has your information), mobile deposit, electronic linkups for online shopping, etc.

Banks are not a good source of startup money. It's not their job. They are better at financing ongoing operations. You'll want to have a demonstrable "good citizen" track record in place before that first real money meeting. Build your track record with a bank you like, starting now.

TIP

I am personally very fond of credit unions. Many offer exceptional rates and personal service that can be hard to find at big banks. Don't discount them when you're looking for a financial institution.

LEGAL

Everyone's circumstances will include a greater or lesser need to lawyer up your enterprise from the beginning. There are simple, low cost ways to do the initial registration stuff online. This is ideal for a single person as owner. For most of us, we may not need much more lawyering at this stage of our enterprises. When you add a second person as an owner (please don't tell me you're friends and nothing can go wrong), you need to get advice from an attorney. The problem is not how you are going to get INTO business together, the problem is how you're going to get OUT of business should that become necessary. For other people with more complicated financial lives, see your lawyer for advice on organizing your startup.

Law firms are businesses, too. They need new prospects in their customer pool just like everyone else. Even if you can organize and register

Ageless Entrepreneur Spotlight

Estella Pyfrom, founder and CEO of Estella's Brilliant Bus and
2015 Purpose Prize Fellow (Florida)

Q: *How did you find your current passion?*

A: At age 71, when most people are settling down after working and serving their communities during a lifetime, I was just beginning my second career. I entered into the field of technology and created Estella's Brilliant Bus.

Q: *What would you do differently now that you've had some time developing your current adventure?*

A: My adventure serving the underserved communities continues to be very gratifying.

I understand that the population my organization serves doesn't have very many resources, but they are blessed with the ability to share their love for each other, which is what keeps us all motivated to continue to move forward. If I had to live my life all over again, I would not change anything. I am truly thankful for all of the life experiences I had during my journey to year 81 in my adventurous life.

Q: *What is the best piece of advice you would share with someone in the second half of life considering entrepreneurship?*

A: My advice to anyone who is considering a second life considering entrepreneurship is not to be afraid to dream. Dream big. Believe in your dreams, and know that you can achieve your dreams—if you are willing to work to make your dreams come true. Life over 55 can be very rewarding, and at age 81 and beyond, you still have a lot to offer and can make a difference in the lives of many people . . . So give your community the best that you have, and the best will come back to you. Be inspired, and go for it.

your business without a lawyer, you'd better be thinking about finding one you'd like to work with, should it become necessary. Talk to a few. Most will explain their fees and requirements without charge. It can't hurt.

If you want you and your business to be sustainable, then build in good bones from the beginning: accounting, insurance, data management, banking, and legal.

This is NOT an unnecessary paper-pushing exercise slowing your ascent into lofty entrepreneurial heights. Without good bones, your new enterprise becomes one more thing causing problems in your life.

Build in good bones from the start. Done right, your own sustainable enterprise is your way out of those problems.

CHAPTER 6 DELIVERABLES

Many of us dream of running our own small enterprises. It's easy to imagine the support and freedoms this lifestyle might generate. Being an entrepreneur is a cool prospect, and putting yourself into that picture can bring hope. But long before you get to the fun stuff, you need to put in place the "good bones" that you can build a viable structure around. Ageless startups have a better chance than most to make valuable contributions to their owners as well as to the communities they serve, but without professional support services, you are putting your contributions at risk. Do the grunt work yourself wherever you can, but then go find people providing these services to verify and finalize your work. Remember:

- ▶ *Good bones first.* Your business won't survive reliable management systems in place.
- ▶ *CPA for the win.* Accounting is a huge daily task. After all, you want to make money and be sure that you keep it. Choose your CPA with care.
- ▶ *Insure, insure, insure.* Yes, you need insurance to cover both your assets and your income. Don't skimp on this one—buy the insurance that will help you sleep at night.
- ▶ *Keep it data driven.* Track it all—your customers, potential clients, vendors, and sales leads. It doesn't matter what you use to store

and manage your data, as long as you create a system that works for you.

▸ *Leave legal to the lawyers.* From the first day you sign paperwork for your business entity to the day you pass your legacy on to your heirs, a lawyer will help you through the massive forest of legal issues.

At this point, you've got a plan, a team of experts to rely on, and a systematic way to manage your startup. But now, you've got to sell it. In the next chapter, we'll talk marketing and how you can set yourself apart with your expertise.

MARKETING YOUR AGELESS STARTUP

A s ageless entrepreneurs, our highest calling is to pass on wisdom.

I'm still learning that now. Working on the coolest startup of my life, my main goal is to pass on what I learn and to hand off whatever wisdom I've accumulated to the next generations.

Does wisdom mean you excel at doing this? No. No one entrepreneur excels at every task they take on in their business. But wisdom has taught me that there are some functions your business cannot do without, like marketing. And one great advantage you have as an ageless entrepreneur is that you can not only market your product or service, but your wisdom as an industry veteran.

When you are marketing and selling your ageless startup, keep in mind that it's not just the specific product or service you are selling. You are selling wisdom. In this chapter, you will learn to see the value of your work is not just the growth of your own enterprise, but is also the sharing of wisdom.

BELIEVE (AND CREATE) BETTER STORIES

As an ageless entrepreneur, you have the high ground. You can speak from a position of knowledge, know-how, and networks. You can tell an authentic story honed from experience. You are in a position to be a truth-teller, regardless of how it is received. Your age and your knowledge bring authenticity.

Nothing else will work. Everything else will ultimately fail. Period. You have to approach your enterprise with that attitude, or you're toast. In the short term, of course, you can fool a few people, but it's not sustainable.

The need to be authentic with yourself is equally critical. You need to follow your own common sense and honor your insight when you've found the contribution you can make. You do not need to fit into other people's views of how your enterprise should look. Plan it to match your own skills. Excluding the IRS, do not automatically accept any rules for participating in startups and emerging enterprises.

For ageless startups, led by people with knowledge and networks, there has never been a better time to utilize your wisdom to tell a valuable story to the markets that need your insight.

If you launch an ageless startup, the stories you tell will strongly influence your outcomes. Make your own story vivid and valuable because nobody—*nobody*—can tell it better than you can. Ignore the pitches and the fast answers. Sure, there are lessons to be learned from many directions, but your way forward is your story to write.

As ageless entrepreneurs, we have the advantage of time on our side. We have lived through a wide variety of experiences, troubles, and triumphs. We know what has worked, and more importantly, what hasn't. We don't need to be afraid of the opinions of others. We don't need fame or adulation. We do need to pass on wisdom.

We need to leave a legacy.

When you tell your story, don't lean on the specifics. There will be time for that as your conversations with stakeholders develop. To introduce yourself and define your work, look to the higher levels of what you are bringing to the table and how your solutions are designed for lasting value. The benefits we bring to our work are rooted in leadership and longevity, not in short-term gain. There are significant experience-based advantages developed over time that we bring to the world as ageless entrepreneurs.

Get yourself a blank piece of paper. Ask yourself hard questions, and write down the answers:

▸ How does my previous life's work position me to be a leader in my chosen niche?

▸ What gives me the authority to lead discussions about the future of the industry or market I want to serve?

▸ How can my work lead others to better outcomes for their organizations and the lives they touch?

▸ How has my work and life experience informed my judgment today? Why is that important to others?

▸ What changes in my target markets have I seen over time? What's worked? What turned out to be a dead end?

▸ How does the work I did before this inform what comes next for those I propose to serve?

It can be valuable to phrase these answers as stories. Stories drive life. Stories prepare others for the future. Stories nurture confidence and courage. You have those stories in your life history. Share them with others. Give back. Pay it forward. Lead. Create a better world for those who follow.

Remember, the story is about YOU. Your ageless startup is built around you. Your life experiences are what matter to the listener. You have led a unique and valuable life no matter the circumstances. You have wisdom and experience and know-how that is specific to you. Be confident. Let people know what brought you to the point you are at in your life. You are not doing mass-marketing, you are creating human-to-human connections that will build a community of interest around your enterprise. How does your life inform your business mission? What values do you bring to your enterprise? How does the knowledge you've developed over your life translate into business goals that will bring value to your customers? You are here to pass on your wisdom and make the world better. The world wants to know you. This is your chance to introduce yourself.

Write it down. Then believe it. Then do it.

Ageless Entrepreneur Spotlight

Dr. Pat Wolff, founder of Meds & Food for Kids and
2013 Purpose Prize Fellow (Missouri)

Q: *How did you find your current passion?*

A: I first began volunteering on medical missions to poverty-stricken Haiti in 1988 with my two young children in tow. For 15 years, I worked to alleviate sickness and hunger, which is especially brutal on Haiti's children. I lost count of the number of children I saw die.

Q: *Are there any mistakes you can share from your own current career?*

A: We should have set up the factory as a commercial entity. It is now awkwardly a nonprofit. This causes perceptual and legal problems for us in Haiti.

Q: *What is the best piece of advice you would share with someone in the second half of life considering entrepreneurship?*

A: Be persistent. Don't be afraid to fail. All failure is relative, and it can be the starting point for the next project. Work hard. Engage others in your vision. You might have to modify the plan, but there is always some way to get around the obstruction. Don't get complacent. Stay a little scared. Hope for the best. Plan for the worst.

NAIL THE ELEVATOR PITCH

When your enterprise is up and running, all kinds of people will ask you what you do. You need a short, sweet, drive-by answer.

Potential customers, bankers, potential investors, community development folks, and neighbors will all ask. That's just the start.

As a startup or emerging enterprise, you know damn well that what you do is as varied as the weather and twice as unpredictable. My advice: Don't use that for your answer.

Yes, you need a story. But you also need the movie trailer to your story. You need to explain your story and your work as though your enterprise depended on it. It just might.

No one wants an answer that provides the mission statement delivered with unnecessary humor, angst, or doubt thrown in.

TIP

What do you do? Your elevator pitch answer needs to be a few really great words. The fewer, the better.

The ones that you really want to understand your answer are potential customers. To interest most potential customers, you've got three or four seconds. You need to be smart, fast, and accurate.

Others will need to hear your short answer, so they can ask more intelligent questions from their perspectives. They don't want to hear your full story up-front. They have their own stories they're busy working on. If you want their help, you'd better participate by keeping your answer short so they can see how your enterprise fits in with theirs.

So, what do you do? Keep your answer short and smart. Make it enthusiastic and accurate. Then, when someone asks what you do, be polite and blurt it out.

I think the best answers are either questions or answers that lead your listener into asking a question. My current favorite is from an amazing tech company founded by a couple of brothers from a rural village in Ireland. Their company, Stripe, is currently conquering the online payment world. When asked what they do, the founders don't say they write software. They say, "We increase the GDP of the internet."

Tony Robbins, the famous life and business strategist, says simply, "I get you to be the man or woman you were meant to be."

Camp Lone Hollow says, "Texas' premiere summer camp for boys and girls. Unplugged and unforgettable."

Businesses and organizations solve problems, or they won't continue to exist. Consider answering "What do you do?" with a question focusing on the problems you help solve. "You know those problems we all have keeping our computers up to date? I fix that."

Practice this skill, and your business practice will grow with you.

TELL THE TRUTH

The best salesperson I ever hired had never worked in sales before.

My business partner and I met the prospect for breakfast. I told my partner that I would take it slow and leave plenty of time for consideration. We were still looking at the breakfast menu, just one or two coffees into it, when I offered the prospect the job. My partner just shook his head.

Our potential new sales manager, Dan, had asked just what the sales job description entailed. Dan had not worked in sales previously. He thought it sounded great but, well, what's the deal? What do you need to do for a sales job?

If your enterprise is to be sustainable, you can't build it on lies. You can never shortchange your product or service. You need to be the best at something, but never overpromise your way into defeat. You can't

 Ageless Entrepreneur Spotlight

Jane Burns, entrepreneur (Wisconsin)

Q: *How did you find your current passion?*

A: I think what sort of stirred me finally and ultimately to action was the continued exasperation with the work world. I often say, "I'm not tired of working; I am tired of the work world," meaning a revolving door of co-workers, supervisors, office politics, worrying about layoffs, bureaucracy, etc. Then I realized in some ways, I did have the power to possibly do something about that because I have an idea. And even if my idea didn't bring me money, it would bring me a joy and a sense of self-determination that I was no longer getting from my professional life.

Q: *What would you do differently now that you've had some time developing your current adventure?*

A: DIVE IN EARLIER. I mulled the idea for way too long, and while I don't think I lost my chance, I saw others come to this same conclusion and start hosting similar events. It won't wreck my idea, but some of these are places/groups I had targeted as potential clients, and they figured it out by themselves without me pitching my product/services to them.

And it was only by doing that I realized this was making me happier than my actual job. That's a big thing I missed out on while letting the idea live in my brain far too long.

Q: *What is the best piece of advice you would share with someone in the second half of life considering entrepreneurship?*

A: Tell people about your idea. I was given this advice early, and it sounds counterintuitive but it is really true. If it's an invention, people aren't going to have the same knowledge you have and aren't going to run home and invent the same thing. If it's a service you are creating to meet a need, generally the whole point is that you thought of it and have some research and work behind it that someone isn't going to run home and whip up in an hour and beat you to the punch.

Also, by telling people about my idea, I got my first customer—someone I never would have found on my own. Someone else knew what I was creating and introduced me. When she told me what it was she was looking for; it was like she was reading my business goals out loud. Telling people about your idea also means that everyone else will have ideas about what you should do, so you have to navigate that politely. Some might be good; some might be bad. It's kind of like when you buy a house and everyone who sees it tells you how you should decorate, and you just nod politely.

under-deliver. You can't execute poorly and survive. Every single thing in your operation needs full transparency, repeatability, and grand-slam data control. Above all, you need honesty in your data and honesty in your life.

Starting honorable, well-executed, and properly documented, new enterprises looks hard. The reality is that it's far easier than wading into the world of cheating and lies. That stuff always takes far more time, work, and effort than doing things right.

Before we had a chance to order breakfast, I told Dan his sales training came in a package of three words: tell the truth.

He said, "I can do that," and we shook on the deal.

Enterprise is full of risk. Minimize it. But if you want to participate, you're going to have to prepare, then learn to live with it.

Was there risk in hiring Dan? Sure.

Was there reward in hiring Dan? Immediately.

Why? Because Dan succeeded for all of us by minimizing risks.

How does he do that? By telling the truth. That's a core tenant of any sustainable business practice.

BUILD MOMENTUM

Momentum is the best friend a sustainable enterprise (and a marketer) can have. Organizing your business model and your sales channels to encourage repeat orders is your goal.

There are no better sales prospects than existing customers. This isn't always possible and not all customers will behave, but the more you can build in repeaters, the more sustainable your operation becomes.

Case in point: For many years, we sold banners to local service clubs through their parent organizations. Users out at the end of the food chain saw value in what we offered and built in repeat purchases of our stuff for their special events come rain, shine, or revolution.

One of our best examples of this was a rush order we were asked to produce for a pancake breakfast in Paramaribo, Suriname, located on the northeast tip of South America. The only problem was that it had to be delivered by express air that Saturday. It seemed that a revolution was underway. Insurgents were expected to control the airport by Monday, and no one knew what would happen by Tuesday.

So what did they do in their besieged capital city with armed conflict and political chaos all around? Same thing as last year. Throw another pancake breakfast and order the banners.

Whatever you do in your sustainable work life, try to build in repeat orders from existing customers.

Momentum. Build it into your practice.

BE A COLD-CALLING SUPERSTAR

"Nothing happens until somebody sells something." This famous quote is attributed to a number of people, including Peter Drucker and IBM's Thomas Watson.

When we are young, everyone and everything seems bigger, smarter, and more daunting than they really are.

Sure, there is a valuable brashness inherent in the young, but it's usually driven by enthusiasm—not experience. Enthusiasm is important, but it can only get you so far in today's market.

What is more sustainable as an approach to sales and marketing is experience. Wisdom, experience, and solutions always outweigh enthusiasm alone.

Cold calls—the initial contact with a potential new customer—used to be a game of raw numbers. You would work to see how many contacts you could make so that some small percentage could eventually emerge as viable business partners and customers.

The new approach, a much better and more valuable one for those with years of experience, is the cold call that seeks to provide solutions and opportunities based on your own experience.

When looking for possible customers, look for organizations within your field that are growing. These are most often the kind of places where they are creating their own new opportunities and are receptive to suggested solutions.

Follow these groups on their social media sites. Search out new publications and announcements on their web site or in the media.

Search out individuals within that organization who seem to be quoted often or who are out front on social media. Ask to join their networks on professional networking sites such as LinkedIn. Follow their work. Get to know their approach to growth and development. Keep a running note on each of them in your database or however you're organizing yourself.

When you think you have a good working understanding of these individuals and their companies, reach out to them. If it is remotely by email or phone, let them know you haven't yet met but you have been

 Ageless Entrepreneur Spotlight

David Wolf, cofounder of The Campaign for College Opportunity and 2015 Purpose Prize Fellow (California)

Q: *Are there any mistakes you can share from your own current career?*

A: These are not so much "mistakes" as late-arriving realizations. First, even as well-connected at Steve and I were as a result of our paying careers, we had to keep modifying our thinking as new players and perspectives were brought to our attention. So, we learned to avoid getting wed to any fixed notions about a "plan" or approach and ultimately injected a great deal of dynamism into the ongoing operation. Second, we came to greatly respect and learn from the young people we hired. They had ideas and an energy that we did not have, and ultimately our experience and their brilliance proved a good combination.

Q: *What is the best piece of advice you would share with someone in the second half of life considering entrepreneurship?*

A: If something is bothering you about the state of the world, think about your assets and what you can bring to an effort to make things better. Don't wait. Pay no attention to risk analysis; if you fail, you fail, but know you gave it a shot. (Steve and I ultimately created five non-profits to combat various major problems, and two of them were not very successful—but we learned a great deal through the process.)

admiring how their organization is working and contributing to the world. Ask if you might contribute by sending information about yourself and your service or product.

Better yet, when you've gathered enough knowledge about the organization, ask if you can meet in person at their workplace or at a conference if that's available. In both cases, remotely or in person, refer to publications or initiatives the target organization has released and why you think those are important.

Be able to quickly define the value proposition you are bringing to them: why you can help and how you can help. What is unique about you and your offer? You're not selling them something. You're there to help the good efforts the organization is already making.

Fawning over people never works. Being smart about their work always does. Nobody likes to be sold, but everyone likes to buy. Make it easy for them to see the difference.

People want to learn. Be the great teacher we all remember.

Cold calls for ageless entrepreneurs should be approached as opportunities to share your knowledge and insight in ways that make those you are approaching see new opportunities for themselves to solve problems they have in their own lives and organizations.

You're not relying on enthusiasm to wear someone down. You're relying on experience to lift them up.

PRACTICE PERSISTENCE

I read a great interview with John McPhee in the *New Yorker* in their October 3, 2005 issue.

McPhee is a Pulitzer Prize winner, author of 29 books, with awards and accolades from a zillion directions. He also continues to teach writing at Princeton University well into his 70s.

McPhee noted that making your own gig doesn't have to involve making widgets. It involves making contributions.

You can do it with your own unique talents and skills. You don't need Pulitzer Prizes, and neither does Mr. McPhee. The most valuable trait you need to develop is persistence.

As the interview ended, Mr. McPhee was talking about all the pitches he'd made to the *New Yorker* over the course of ten years, trying to break in. He'd wanted to write for them since he was a teenager. First ignored, then rejected, he kept pitching. That turned into rejections with notes attached. That's when he started closing in. He offered deals, like working on spec.

John McPhee didn't get cautious. McPhee broke the rules. He pitched an idea they specifically told him they did not want. McPhee not only pitched it, but buried them in pitch—with a 5,000-word letter telling his lifelong target customer why they were wrong and why his never-published-in-their-magazine ideas should prevail. And that landed him the gig, with many more to follow, allowing him to work as a writer full-time.

Persistence is one of those gritty attributes that is rarely mythologized, yet in the world of small enterprise it is perhaps the single biggest predictor of success. You will be told "no" repeatedly. You will face misunderstanding and worse. Sure, things will turn out to be memories that never came to fruition. The trick is to see "no" as an opportunity. "No" is a question. Why not? What's better? What can I learn from this? How can I do this differently next time?

In an environmental business I started a while back, I was told repeatedly by investors, bankers, vendors, and even potential customers that my idea wouldn't work. Some thought it was a design problem. Some thought it was a materials problem, and others thought it was simply the wrong approach. I improved our designs, materials, and approaches but kept to the core solution that everyone seemed to doubt. I finally found a potential customer that would let me try because the problem we were addressing had become so acute at their plant. Some of those predictions came true. Designs, materials, and approaches needed improvements, but the idea was sound. We pounded through and kept tinkering until we conquered the problem. Then we marched on and did it over and over across the globe.

TIP

Whatever your enterprise, whatever your endeavor, whatever your contribution, there will be tough, difficult times. Planning and executing minimizes that stuff, but nothing substitutes for persistence and risk-taking with honor.

It wasn't the novel intellectual property that won the day. It wasn't my sales work. It wasn't any one thing except persistence.

I keep a great quote on the subject of persistence pinned to my office wall, often attributed to Calvin Coolidge, but which has earlier origins.

Nothing in this world can take the place of persistence. Talent will not: nothing is more common than unsuccessful men with talent. Genius will not: unrewarded genius is almost a proverb. Education will not: the world is full of educated derelicts. Persistence and determination alone are omnipotent.

Risk-taking in the life of any enterprise should be considered a sport. Good entrepreneurs work to avoid risk that can damage their work. The best ones I know practice smart risk-taking that improves their work incrementally. Like any sport, it requires mastery of the little things before you can achieve a high level of success. Risk small things often in service of greater things. It is like muscle memory. The more you practice it, the more it grows in strength and ability.

Stupid risk-taking in business is a death march. Betting the farm on a home run is a game you never want to be in.

As entrepreneurs, risk will always be with us no matter how hard we try to avoid it. Creating something new requires risk.

A myth of startups is one of entrepreneurs persisting *through* risk, no matter the consequences. That rarely works. Persistence down a dead end is a rookie mistake. Effective entrepreneurs are persistent in *assessing* risk. We constantly monitor the landscape for changing variables that affect our risk profile. We are persistent in our job of reducing risk and increasing value.

Good business practice is based on generating value, telling great stories, and making smart persistence the heart of your practice.

CHAPTER 7 DELIVERABLES

So, how can you market? Simple—tell your story. You have knowledge, know-how, and networks that you can use to make the world a better place. You have a unique story, value, and meaning. You have stories you can share to inspire potential customers. Stories keep the world going around. Sales and marketing for ageless entrepreneurs should focus on sharing truth, expertise, and stories:

▶ *Sell wisdom.* You have lived through profound changes in history. You've seen many things that didn't work, along with many that did, so share it.

▶ *Know your elevator pitch cold.* What's your story? Be able to tell it succinctly and on demand.

▶ *Market your ability to solve problems.* "I'll fix that" is what customers want to hear.

▶ *Tell the truth.* This mantra is the key to your sales success. If you tell the truth about your product or service, you've won the customer.

▶ *Rely on referrals.* There are no better sales prospects than existing customers, so get them involved in your marketing efforts.

▶ *Use your lifetime of skills to sell your startup.* Ageless entrepreneurs are best at cold calls, so jump in and start dialing.

▶ *Your expertise is your ticket to a marketing plan that pays dividends.* Be the great teacher everyone remembers—show potential customers, current clients, and other stakeholders that you know your stuff.

Marketing isn't hard, but it may be new to you. That's okay. As an ageless entrepreneur, you already have a marketing mentality—now, you just need to tap into it to reach your audience. That kind of boldness, to get out there and market a brand-new startup—is what makes you the expert in your chosen field. It also makes you a leader. That's what we'll cover next: how you can lead your startup and secure your legacy as an ageless entrepreneur.

LEADING YOUR LEGACY

During difficult times—and you will face difficult times—it will be tempting to change important parts of your business in reaction to stressful events of the day.

You have written down your mission, your values, and your goals in your business plan. You will make changes to the execution of your plan over time that have been merited through testing and experience, but the mission, values, and goals will be there to guide you.

When struggling through difficult situations, I find it to be an ideal time to revisit your mission and your values and to use them to guide your judgement when reacting to the troubles of the day.

As a small-business owner and entrepreneur who has fought through these miserable spells in the past, I can honestly and enthusiastically say that sticking to the bedrock of mission and values will guide you through better than any spur-of-the-moment, opportunistic decision-making you are tempted to try. Go to your bedrock mission, and tie your anchor there during tough times. This is your safe harbor. As an ageless entrepreneur, you have the benefit of already having served in some kind of leadership position. Now, in this chapter, let's walk through how you can maximize your existing leadership experience for your ageless startup by identifying the essence of leadership, looking back on your experience, and learning how to lead with confidence (which sometimes means saying "no").

 Ageless Entrepreneur Spotlight

Karen Kalish, founder and executive director of Home Works!
The Teacher Home Visit Program and 2015 Purpose Prize Fellow (Missouri)

Q: *What would you do differently now that you didn't do when you started your first nonprofit?*

A: I would NEVER do anything alone, which is what I did when I started Operation Understanding DC, and I made every mistake in the book. It's a miracle that it's still around. Doing things alone is the weakest form of leadership. You must have others to work with, to bounce ideas off of, and to get the work done.

Q: *Are there any mistakes or lessons you can share from starting any of your nonprofits?*

A: Always listen to all voices, especially the naysayers. You learn the most from them.

Always hold up the mirror to yourself when things aren't going well and ask yourself, "What part did I play in this?" Only after you've answered that question can you turn to others.

Always be inclusive of all voices. Always look at IMPACT and have outside evaluation of your work. Numbers are not impact. Number of books read, number of shots given, number of meals served—these are not impact. They are numbers. What *happened* as a result of these actions? Always manage to outcomes.

Bring in outside, independent evaluation and learn from evaluations what to do and not do to be even more effective.

Q: *What is the best piece of advice you would share with someone in the second half of life considering entrepreneurship?*

A: Go on a listening tour FIRST. The world may not need/want yet another nonprofit. Go on a listening tour to see what's out there and what part you can play in nonprofits that already exist. Whatever you want to do is not about you—the entrepreneur. It is about your community and what it needs. Always think about succession—moving on. Founders do not have the same skills as those who maintain or who take nonprofits to the next level. Get out after five to seven years—do not even be on the board. Let new eyes and ears take over, and they don't need a founder looking over their shoulder telling them how to do things or how things have been done. Start it, get it financially healthy, use outside data collection that reflects impact and outcomes, and then turn it over.

THE ESSENCE OF LEADERSHIP

I've launched C corporations, S corporations, LLCs, sole proprietorships, and nonprofits.

And the one thing that sets a leader apart is structure, structure, structure. It defines a lot of what works and what doesn't once the rubber meets the road.

This is not a discourse on legal structures, however. Structures don't make organizations work; leaders do.

I've been thinking about what connects leadership across all the kinds of enterprises that I've had the opportunity to participate in.

A leadership quote that has long inspired me as a lifelong entrepreneur is widely attributed to Woodrow Wilson: "You are not here merely to make a living. You are here in order to enable the world to live more amply, with greater vision, with a finer spirit of hope and achievement. You are here to enrich the world, and you impoverish yourself if you forget the errand."

So, don't forget the errand. Remember that your people are your customers, vendors, stakeholders, and family. Can your work bring value to these collaborations? Can you lead by helping others to grow?

If you are a person considering a startup or working in an emerging enterprise, you need to be a leader, no matter your specific position. The world needs your solutions, and you need to get those solutions deployed. If you are leading a small team or even if you are only leading yourself, you need to create states of mind and actions that help people get better through natural, reproducible, and sustainable solutions.

LOOK BACK SO YOU CAN LEAD GOING FORWARD

In significant new ways, large and small, you have the ability to organize custom sets of skills and the information needed to alleviate real human problems in ways that have never before been possible in human history.

This doesn't mean you need to cure cancer. It means you can make some unique subset of the world a better place. You can organize that effort in ways that are profitable and deliver increased levels of personal self-control.

No, it's not easy. You probably won't get rich. That's the tough news. But yes, there is opportunity everywhere. And yes, you're capable of starting your own enterprise. That's the good news.

Working smart and working hard to provide sustainable solutions has been the business of most people in most societies since the dawn of time.

Despite the trappings, now is no different—except that we have better and cheaper tools than have ever been available in human history. High tech headlines tantalize would-be entrepreneurs, but I think they also deter most of us. That's unfortunate. The simple human skills of basic, sustainable entrepreneurship get thrown out for the false realities of spreadsheets and get-rich seminars.

If ever there was a time to reclaim and celebrate small-scale, sustainable entrepreneurship and all the common sense that entails, now is that time.

But our culture often highlights entrepreneurship and innovation as work that requires seeing into the future. As older entrepreneurs, we can sometime feel walled off from this kind of entrepreneurship. Headlines touting overnight billionaires fill the business press and capture the popular imagination. Entrepreneurship is often framed as dramatic presentations

Ageless Entrepreneur Spotlight

Dori Shimoda, founder of Give Children a Choice and
2012 Purpose Prize Fellow (North Carolina)

Q: *How did you find your current passion?*

A: When on a Citibank business trip to the U.S. (I lived in Belgium at the time), I was 32 and kidnapped for 18 hours at gunpoint. After that experience, I committed to myself that when I was 50 (when my kids would be out of college) that I would give back to help children (our future). I would help either the deaf (because I am deaf and wear aids) or other children with their education. Despite my successful career as SVP of JP Morgan Chase in charge of eCommerce and business transformation for the mortgage business, when I became 50, I began the transition to fulfill my commitment.

Q: *Are there any mistakes you can share from your own current career?*

A: Actually, I've made many mistakes, but mistakes are generally means for improving the next time around.

Q: *What is the best piece of advice you would share with someone in the second half of life considering entrepreneurship?*

A: Have a passion for whatever you do. Passion breeds success. Passion eliminates the "can't do" thinking. Passion transforms "can't do's" to "how will I deal with it?" Think with your passion and brains. Act on your passion.

on television shows aimed at attracting investment. Innovation is usually discussed as a young person's game.

But this is a false wall. The reality is much better. A more inclusive wave of entrepreneurship is opening to those of us in the second half of life. We don't have to work at the bleeding edges of technology to make a difference. We can be leaders in innovating new solutions to problems in our communities and in the markets we know best.

We can lead from experience. We can utilize a lifetime of experience to help. We can look back to find ways forward.

In the world of enterprise, looking back is rarely touted. But looking backward is valuable, given the problems we face today. Many of the skills that got us here are waiting to be re-found. Chief among these are honesty, virtue, hard work, living lean, and optimistic courage.

Looking back brings us to quieter places for ourselves, where we can grow as individuals, enjoy commerce, and contribute to society. Sure, you can use the wonderful, new twenty-first century tools; just learn to use them in ways that support you and the rest of us sustainably. It's easier than you think.

Sustainable work for me means building smart, repeatable business models around common-sense solutions executed with simplicity and, when possible, elegance.

Work hard, stay vigilant, and take small bites. Build your practice on timeless values.

ACTIVATE YOUR LEADERSHIP SKILLS

We ageless entrepreneurs come to the table with lifetimes of struggle, success, failure, and knowledge. We have networks, know-how, and wisdom. We have learned to work with people. We have learned when to change. We have struggled and, at times, succeeded.

We are leaders.

Now it's time to put those leadership skills back into service for the greater good as well as to bring more resilience and security to your life.

Just because you may not have been a CEO or president of anything does not mean you are not a leader. You may have worked on the shipping docks, but you've got a lifetime's worth of experience that others value.

Leaders are people that others turn to for guidance and wisdom.

You can take all of your prior work experience, tie a bow around it, and call it leadership. You don't need permission from anyone. Ask yourself:

▶ What are you proud of?

▶ What did others turn to you for?

▶ How did you solve problems others couldn't?

▶ How did you say no to tasks, people, or activities that did not drive your business forward?

▶ How did you champion ideas that others were missing?

▶ How did you help your co-workers, customers, and vendors when they needed a boost?

Those answers define you as your own unique brand of leader.

And as an ageless entrepreneur, you're free to fly. You're free to walk into appropriate settings and say, "Hi, you don't know me, but I can help."

Real leaders don't seek to be the focus of attention. Leaders seek to focus attention on solving problems.

Ageless entrepreneurs can do this as individuals in a way almost no other cohort in our society can. As an ageless entrepreneur:

▶ You don't need a staff (unless you want one).

▶ You may not need accounting, finance, PR, and marketing department.

▶ You don't have to ask permission and, as a small startup, can move fast and execute nimbly.

▶ You can bring minimum viable products to market while others are stuck in meetings.

▶ You can choose valuable goals.

▶ You can choose honorable strategies.

▶ You can act with ethics, decency, and honesty.

You are a leader on a mission.

KNOW WHEN TO SAY NO

Your life as a new entrepreneur will bring you face-to-face with bad customers. It's a hard spot to be in when you need the business.

Ageless Entrepreneur Spotlight

Laurie Ahern, president of Disability Rights International and
2015 Purpose Prize Fellow (Washington, DC)

Q: *What is your current career path?*

A: My third act was pretty dramatic to me at the time. I was 49 and single. My son was grown and living an independent life. And out of the blue, I get a call from this DC-based nonprofit called Mental Disability Rights International (now called Disability Rights International, or DRI) asking me if I was interested in applying for the position of associate director. (I had never lived anywhere except Massachusetts.) The ED, attorney Eric Rosenthal, suggested I come on a trip with DRI staff and some board members to Uruguay—to conduct a human rights investigation on the rights of people with disabilities and to see firsthand what the organization was truly about. That was 15 years ago. Since then, I have become president of the organization and have worked in countless countries, such as Kosovo, the Republic of Georgia, Ukraine, Kenya, Mexico, and Geneva. I have lived alone in Istanbul, been detained by police in Serbia, and been attacked by hospital guards in Romania. I have written many human rights reports and negotiated with governments, and our work has been featured in newspapers and television around the globe. And I have written pieces for *The Washington Post, The New York Times, The Huffington Post*, and in legal and human rights journals.

Q: *Are there any mistakes you can share from your own current career?*

A: Be very careful when you visit a country after you have criticized their government in a *Washington Post* editorial.

Q: *What is the best piece of advice you would share with someone in the second half of life considering entrepreneurship?*

A: Walk on the wild side, and don't be afraid of taking risks.

As a new entrepreneur, you don't have to take every job or every client that appears. The goal of smart startups is just the opposite.

I turned down a potential client recently even though the money would have been great.

My problem was the client. He was a new economy guy who wanted to start a business in such a way that he could monetize it by automating a website to generate income. He assured me he'd read all the articles about gaming Google algorithms.

Don't get me wrong. I'm a huge believer in using the internet to communicate the stories and values of small enterprises. There has never been a more powerful tool in the history of the world of business.

But this new world of monetizing websites through search engine optimization alone, while having very little content or value, leaves me cold.

I turned down this potential client. They will not be the last.

Successful enterprise is not based on keywords. It's based on problem-solving content.

The world needs startups that solve real problems, not ones that are launched to scam Google algorithms. Improve your content. Continually improve your value. That's real enterprise. That's your practice.

Leaders create opportunities. Leaders assess opportunities based on creating value for their customers and their communities.

Leaders know when to say no. You are a leader.

THE VALUE OF DOING OVER DAYDREAMING

What's getting me a bit nuts is the preponderance of media shouting out that you need to follow your bliss into entrepreneurship. In other words, you need to do it—not just dream it.

Yes, I agree. But then what? Do you follow your bliss over a cliff? At least you'd enjoy the plunge for a few short moments. If you are going to thrive in your small business, you have to have all the parts of your mind and body engaged.

I love the quote from Dr. Howard Thurman, the great religious leader and pioneering civil rights activist who mentored Dr. Martin Luther King Jr.:

Don't ask yourself what the world needs. Ask yourself what makes you come alive, and go do that, because what the world needs is people who have come alive.

Did that mean Dr. Thurman spent his days navel-gazing? Just the opposite. He wrote more than 20 books. He met Mahatma Gandhi and, at Gandhi's request, brought back his message of non-violence to African Americans, then served as spiritual advisor and mentor to Dr. Martin Luther King Jr.'s family. He gave up a safe, honored, and tenured faculty position to change the world.

He worked relentlessly, as though tomorrow really needed him. It did. However, it's the DOING of the work that matters, not the thinking about it.

Yes, you REALLY do need to love what you do, but not because you'll be following your bliss. You need to love what you do because you'll be living with your work through times of miserable cash flow, angry customers, crushing time constraints, and working more hours than you can imagine.

That doesn't sound like following your bliss. It's not. What really matters is working toward your bliss.

You mean it's hard? More than I could tell you. *You mean it's going to take longer than I think?* Yes.

Does that mean you shouldn't do it?

Just the opposite. You need to enter commerce, as have thousands of generations before you, and work hard and solve problems. Keep excellent notes and records, and then work harder to make it all happen again and again and again.

Doing what you love is critical. The key word is *doing*. Not talking about it but acting in an efficient way, creating sustainable (reproducible) business models around what you love. Trying, failing, trying again, and above all else, showing up every day.

Then, and only then, will you be able to turn your bliss into a business.

TIP

Small business startups are like making meat loaf. You've got to plunge in. You've got to commit to mixing up improbable ingredients. You've got to clean up the resulting mess. The process is not automated or done without effort. Yet the results can be wonderful and nourish you well beyond the event.

Ageless Entrepreneur Spotlight

Joe Bute, founder of Hollymead Capital (Pennsylvania)

Q: *How did you find your ageless career?*

A: I always wanted to actually run a business rather than just invest in one. So, when I went off to try and raise a small fund to invest in food businesses in 2015, we found Tomanetti's. It was smaller than even I thought was practical, but I figured we had to start somewhere. So, I found three investors and two partners, and we bought the company. The rest, as they say, is history.

Q: *What would you do differently as an ageless entrepreneur?*

A: I think I would like to have had more resources in my pocket when I started. Unfortunately, I basically burned through all of my savings trying to get to this point, which means I had no margin for error and spent a lot of time trying to figure out how to make personal financial ends meet. It would be a lot more fun if I didn't have to look for spare change in the sofa every night.

Q: *Are there any mistakes you can share from your own encore career?*

A: Tons. Along the same lines as above, try to make sure you are not trying to make the business work while you are trying to pay your bills. Another is never underestimate how hard it is to run any business—size is not much of a differentiation. Small is just as complicated as big in the world of business—it just doesn't pay as well, and there is a lot less room for error.

Q: *What is your best piece of advice you would share with someone in the second half of life considering entrepreneurship?*

A: Always do what you love, have passion for it, and lower your expectations regarding financial return—if it isn't fun to go to work, then don't do it.

CHAPTER 8 DELIVERABLES

The world needs you. You may not have all the answers, but you have solutions that are unique to you. Leading and launching new enterprises to share those solutions is the goal of this work. As a leader, you can move the world forward in many ways, both small and large. The work can be messy and difficult, but you've been there and done that. How can you honor that experience by sharing it with others? Your own small enterprise can be the structure you need to share your wisdom and experience. Your leadership matters. Give it a home. Remember:

- ▶ *Your mission, values, and goals will guide you.* These three elements are your collective North Star. When in doubt, leaders will revisit these driving forces to reset and renew their business.
- ▶ *Focus outward.* Lead by helping others to grow and meet their own goals. Doing so helps you foster a sense of community and showcases your leadership skills in your own company and in your community.
- ▶ *Think long term.* Organize your new enterprise to provide lasting value for all of your stakeholders: customers, vendors, partners, employees, and your family.
- ▶ *Remember that this isn't a fairy tale.* Be ready to forego bliss for hard work. Your business isn't in charge of your personal happiness—you are.

Show up every day. Being present is both a literal and figurative mindset. Show up physically, mentally, and emotionally to give your business your best. Act like a leader, and you will be one.

PARTING THOUGHTS

In this book, we have explored the themes of giving yourself permission to learn more, planning an enterprise that works on your terms, and building a professional practice no matter the field you choose.

Ageless Startup is designed to be an exploration of entrepreneurship in the second half of life. You have the ability to launch your own enterprise, to put your skills to work in service to your community and to generate additional income and independence for yourself. *Ageless Startup* is also a strategy for creating a new career you can carry into the second half of life on your own terms, generating personal income, and creating a legacy of help and support for the ideas, communities, and markets you are passionate about. The world needs you. You have led a life that has endowed you with unique knowledge, know-how, and networks. Your life experiences are valuable to others.

This is the renaissance age of entrepreneurship, and it's just beginning. You do not have to follow conventional models. You can build a business that meets your needs and one that is done on your terms. More than half of older workers face the prospect of being pushed out of longtime jobs before they choose to retire. *Ageless Startup* is designed help you make a smooth transition from working for someone else to working for yourself. You can do this in ways that minimize your risk and maximize your value, while building business systems that keep you on track.

You are not alone. Older entrepreneurs represent the fastest growing segment of the startup world. The enterprises you launch can be specific to your needs and don't need to meet anyone else's needs but your own. Of the 32 million businesses in the U.S., 25 million are solo entrepreneurs. You can become part of one of the biggest stories of our time.

Start small. Start smart. Start right now. It's not hard. It's just new.

RESOURCES FOR AGELESS ENTREPRENEURS

STATE-BY-STATE RESOURCES
Alabama

Alabama Launch Pad
www.alabamalaunchpad.com

Alabama Entrepreneurial Institute at the Culverhouse College of Business
https://aei.culverhouse.ua.edu/

Alabama Small Business Development Center Network
www.asbdc.org

Alaska

Alaska Department of Commerce
www.commerce.alaska.gov

Anchorage Economic Development Corporation
www.aedcweb.com

Alaska Small Business Development Center
www.aksbdc.org

Arizona

Center for Entrepreneurial Innovation
www.ceigateway.com

Arizona State University Entrepreneurship + Innovation Program
https://.entrepreneurship.asu.edu

Arizona Women's Education and Entrepreneur Center
www.aweecenter.org

Arkansas

Arkansas Economic Development Commission
www.arkansasedc.com

Arkansas Capital Corporation
www.arcapital.com

California

California Governor's Office of Business and Economic Development
www.business.ca.gov

California Business Portal Innovation and Entrepreneurship Unit
http://businessportal.ca.gov/business-assistance/entrepreneurship/

University of California Office of Innovation and Entrepreneurship
www.ucop.edu/innovation-entrepreneurship/

Colorado

Colorado Office of Economic Development and International Trade
www.choosecolorado.com

Colorado Small Business Development Center
www.coloradosbdc.org

Connecticut

Connecticut Center for Entrepreneurship and Innovation
www.ccei.uconn.edu

Connecticut Department of Economic and Community Development
https://portal.ct.gov/DECD

Delaware

Delaware Division of Small Business
www.business.delaware.gov

Delaware First
https://delawarefirst.udel.edu/priorities/innovation-entrepreneurship/

Horn Entrepreneurship at University of Delaware
www.udel.edu/research-innovation/horn/

Florida

Enterprise Florida Small Business Portal
www.enterpriseflorida.com/small-business/

Warrington College of Business Entrepreneurship and Innovation Center
https://warrington.ufl.edu/entrepreneurship-and-innovation-center

Florida Department of Economic Opportunity
www.floridajobs.org

Georgia

Georgia Department of Economic Development Small Business Portal
www.georgia.org/small-business/start

Georgia State University Entrepreneurship and Innovation Institute
www.eni.gsu.edu

Hawaii

Hawaii Department of Commerce and Community Affairs
http://cca.hawaii.gov/bac/

Hawaii Small Business Development Center
www.hisbdc.org

Hawaii Technology Development Corporation
www.htdc.org/money/

Idaho

Idaho Department of Commerce
www.commerce.idaho.gov

Idaho Small Business Development Center
www.idahosbdc.org

Illinois

Illinois Department of Commerce and Economic Opportunity
Small Business Portal
www2.illinois.gov/dceo/SmallBizAssistance/Pages/default.aspx

Illinois Technology Entrepreneur Center
www.tec.illinois.edu/

Indiana

Indiana Economic Development Corporation Startup Portal
https://iedc.in.gov/startup

Indiana Small Business Development Center
https://isbdc.org/

Iowa

Iowa Secretary of State's Small Business Resource Center
https://sos.iowa.gov/business/StartingABusiness/search.aspx

Iowa Economic Development Targeted Small Business Program
www.iowaeconomicdevelopment.com/tsb

Iowa Small Business Development Center
www.iowasbdc.org

Kansas

Kansas Small Business Development Center
www.kansassbdc.net

Network Kansas
www.networkkansas.com

Kentucky

Kentucky Small Business Development Center
www.ksbdc.org

Women's Business Center of Kentucky
www.wbckentucky.org

Kentucky Innovation Center
www.kyinnovation.com

Louisiana

Louisiana Economic Development
www.opportunitylouisiana.com

Louisiana Small Business Development Center
www.lsbdc.org

Maine

Maine Small Business Portal
www.maine.gov/portal/business/starting.html

Maine Small Business Development Center
  www.mainesbdc.org

Maryland

Maryland Small Business Development Center
  www.mdsbdc.umd.edu

Maryland Business Resources
  https://open.maryland.gov/business-resources/starting-a-business/

Massachusetts

Massachusetts Guide to Starting a Business
  www.mass.gov/guides/starting-a-new-business

Massachusetts Small Business Development Center
  www.msbdc.org

Michigan

Michigan Small Business Development Center
  www.sbdcmichigan.org

University of Michigan Innovate Blue
  www.innovateblue.umich.edu

Minnesota

Minnesota Small Business Assistance Office
  www.mn.gov/deed/business/help/sbao/

Minnesota Employment and Economic Development
  https://mn.gov/deed/

Mississippi

Mississippi Business Resources
  www.ms.gov/Business

Mississippi Small Business Development Center
www.mssbdc.org

Mississippi Development Authority Small Business Resources
www.mississippi.org

Missouri

Missouri Department of Economic Development Small Business and Entrepreneurship Resources
www.ded.mo.gov/business/start-up-entrepreneurship-programs

Missouri Small Business Development Center
https://sbtdc.umkc.edu

Montana

Montana Governor's Office of Economic Development
www.business.mt.gov/Business-Navigator/Start

Montana Secretary of State's Business Services Division
www.sosmt.gov/business/

Montana Small Business Development Center
www.sbdc.mt.gov/

Nebraska

Nebraska Access Business Startup Database Guide
www.nebraskaccess.ne.gov/businessstarting.asp

Nebraska Business Development Center
www.unomaha.edu/nebraska-business-development-center

Nebraska Small Business Startup Guide
www.opportunity.nebraska.gov/start-your-business/

Nevada

Nevada Secretary of State Small Business Guide
www.nvsos.gov/sos/businesses/start-a-business

Nevada Small Business Development Center
www.nevadasbdc.org

New Hampshire

New Hampshire Business Information Portal
www.nh.gov/business/

Stay Work Play New Hampshire
www.stayworkplay.org/work/starting-business-nh/

New Hampshire Small Business Development Center
www.nhsbdc.org

New Jersey

State of New Jersey Business Portal
www.nj.gov/njbusiness/starting

New Jersey Small Business Development Center
https://.njsbdc.com

New Mexico

New Mexico Economic Development and Business Development Resources
www.gonm.biz/business-development/

New Mexico Small Business Development Center
www.nmsbdc.org/

New York

New York State Division of Small Business
https://esd.ny.gov/doing-business-ny/small-business-hub

STARTUP NY Program
www.esd.ny.gov/startup-ny-program

New York Small Business Development Center
www.nyssbdc.org

North Carolina

North Carolina Small Business and Technology Development Center
www.sbtdc.org

North Carolina Small Business Center Network
www.ncsbc.net

North Dakota

North Dakota Small Business Development Center
www.ndsbdc.org

North Dakota Department of Commerce Innovation and Entrepreneurship
www.commerce.nd.gov/services/InnovationEntrepreneurship/

Ohio

Ohio Business Gateway
www.business.ohio.gov

Ohio Development Services Agency—Entrepreneurship and Business Assistance Centers
www.development.ohio.gov/bs/bs_entrepreneurship.htm

Ohio Small Business Development Centers
www.clients.ohiosbdc.ohio.gov

Ohio Office of Small Business and Entrepreneurship
www.development.ohio.gov/bs/bs_sbdc.htm

Oklahoma

Oklahoma Department of Commerce
www.okcommerce.gov

Oklahoma Small Business Development Center
www.oksbdc.org

Oregon

Oregon Business Xpress Startup Toolkit
https://www.oregon.gov/business/Pages/toolkit.aspx

Oregon Business Information Center
http://egov.sos.state.or.us/br/pkg_bc1_web_interview.bic_home

Pennsylvania

Pennsylvania Business One-Stop Shop
www.dced.pa.gov/business-assistance/small-business-assistance/

Pennsylvania Small Business Development Center
www.pasbdc.org

Rhode Island

Rhode Island Department of Commerce Startup Portal
https://commerceri.com/start-my-business/

Rhode Island Department of State Business Quickstart
www.ri.gov/SOS/quickstart/help/

South Carolina

South Carolina Guide to Starting a Business
https://sc.gov/business/starting-business

South Carolina Business One-Stop
www.scbos.sc.gov

South Carolina Small Business Development Center
www.scsbdc.com

South Dakota

South Dakota Business Help
www.sdbusinesshelp.com

South Dakota Small Business Innovative Research Program
www.sbir.gov

Tennessee

Tennessee Department of Economic and Community Development
Business Resources
www.tn.gov/ecd/small-business/bero-home.html

Tennessee Small Business Development Center
www.tsbdc.org

Texas

Texas Economic Development Small Business Programs
www.gov.texas.gov/business/page/small-business-programs

Southwest Texas Border Small Business Development Center Network.
www.txsbdc.org/programs

Texas Small Business Development Center
www.sbdctexas.org

Utah

Utah Business Portal
www.utah.gov/business

Grow Utah
www.growutah.com

Utah Small Business Development Center
www.utahsbdc.org

Vermont

Vermont Small Business Development Center
www.vtsbdc.org

Vermont Corporations and Business Services
www.sec.state.vt.us/corporationsbusiness-services

Virginia

Virginia Small Business Development Center
www.virginiasbdc.org/

Virginia Startup Portal
www.vastartup.org

Virginia Business One-Stop
www.bos.virginia.gov

Washington

Startup Washington
www.startup.choosewashingtonstate.com

Washington Small Business Guide
www.business.wa.gov

Washington Small Business Development Center
www.wsbdc.org

West Virginia

West Virginia One-Stop Business Portal
www.business4.wv.gov

West Virginia Secretary of State's Starting a Business Portal
www.sos.wv.gov/business/Pages/StartWVBus.aspx

West Virginia Small Business Development Center
www.wvsbdc.com

Wisconsin

Wisconsin Economic Development Corporation
www.wedc.org

Wisconsin Technology Council Entrepreneurs' Toolkit
www.wisconsintechnologycouncil.com/entrepreneurs-toolkit

Wisconsin Small Business Development Center
www.wisconsinsbdc.org

Wyoming

Wyoming Business Council Startup Wyoming
www.wyomingbusiness.org/startupwy

Wyoming Small Business Development Center
www.wyomingsbdc.org

ACKNOWLEDGMENTS

I am especially grateful to my wife, Mary Walker. We worked together for decades in the startups discussed in this book, through uncertainty, setbacks, and all the attendant joy. Mary inspired this writing and helped with the early organization of this book. I would not be here without her.

Special thanks to my team at Entrepreneur Press. Editors Jen Dorsey and Danielle Brown helped craft the final outcome with patience, professionalism, and humor. Vanessa Campos taught me to see the value behind this book, for which I'll be forever grateful.

My agent Jeff Herman set all this in motion. Thank you, Jeff.

I am grateful to all the ageless entrepreneurs interviewed in this book. Their determination and grit inspire me to continue to reach higher.

I refer several times to a great book by Chris Anderson, *The Long Tail,* as well as to the books and blog posts of Seth Godin. Thank you, Chris and Seth.

My daughters grew up in a home where entrepreneurship was as ubiquitous as oxygen. I honor them for their love and support and for the wonderful, strong, independent women they have become.

As a lifelong entrepreneur, I acknowledge and thank the countless number of people who have said no to me. They have helped me learn. They have taught me that no is part of the learning curve. They helped me realize that solutions can emerge in countless ways. And to those who said yes along the way, I'm glad we made this book happen together.

ABOUT THE AUTHOR

Rick Terrien learned the lessons of entrepreneurship very early while selling newspapers car-to-car at stoplights. He hasn't stopped creating new business opportunities since.

He was awarded the United States Small Business New Product of the Year by the National Society of Professional Engineers. He has also been recognized by *Fast Company* as one of their Fast 50, now called the World's 50 Most Innovative Companies.

As an innovator, inventor, and business developer with nine U.S. and foreign patents in industrial fluid recycling, his designs have recovered tens of millions of gallons of oil worldwide that were previously lost as wastewater. This equipment has also prevented industrial carbon residues from entering the atmosphere on a globally relevant scale for more than 20 years. His award-winning fluid recycling startup just passed the 20-year mark.

Rick was recognized as a Purpose Prize Fellow in 2015. The Purpose Prize is awarded yearly by AARP to post-retirement individuals who make a difference in industry and innovation by creating new solutions for today's world.

Rick's work as a recognized leader in regional food systems is now over ten years old and gaining momentum. He is currently helping launch and lead one of the most innovative regional food organizations in the world. Rick is a lifelong entrepreneur with an ageless story to share.

INDEX

READER'S NOTES

READER'S NOTES

READER'S NOTES

READER'S NOTES

READER'S NOTES

READER'S NOTES

ARE YOU AN AGELESS ENTREPRENEUR?
Would You Like to Keep Exploring and Learning?

The Center for Ageless Entrepreneurs (CAE) has been established to help you continue your exploration of entrepreneurship in the second half of life.

Based at the Sustainable Enterprise Accelerator at Slippery Rock University, in Slippery Rock, Pennsylvania, USA. The CEA offers monthly webinars with exciting ageless entrepreneurs from all walks of life, working in all manner of fields and markets.

Online, in-depth training programs will also be available, allowing participants to learn at their own speed, on their own schedules. Successful completion will earn a university-based certificate of completion to help with your own launch. Yearly conferences will be held to offer valuable interactions and a place to launch your own ageless startup.

Free Webinars

- Interviews with ageless entrepreneurs from all walks of life.

Online Training and Mentoring Programs

Learn online at your own pace. University-based certificate of completion.

Valuable Yearly Conferences

Meet your peers. Learn from the masters. Launch your own ageless startup here!

For More Information, Visit:

www.agelessentrepreneurs.org